BROKEN FROM PARENT LOSS?

SIMPLE SECRETS OF NAVIGATING GRIEF, BUILDING RESILIENCE, FINDING HOPE & COMFORT AFTER THE LOSS OF YOUR PARENT

ROSETTA FEI

as a result of the use of the information contained within this document, including, but not limited to, — errors, omissions, or inaccuracies.

CONTENTS

A FREE GIFT TO OUR READERS

5 Daily Meditations that you can use to guide you past your grieving. These meditations are very impactful and complement this book to give you comfort, hope and inspiration on your potential to be your best self after losing your loved one. You can download and start using now! Visit this link

https://bit.ly/3dXpPAr

ABOUT THE AUTHOR

Rosetta Fei's interest sparked in grief counselling when she lost her mother when she was about to complete her college degree. The grieving process is different for every individual, and she found it challenging and demanding to cope with the grief and pain from the loss of her parent. She also experienced and dealt with the different stages of grief and went through heartbroken syndrome.

After adjusting to the loss and building resilience, she has grown interested in grief and loss, and other types of emotional pain people may be going through. Rosetta Fei loves to assist those who need help coping with their grief and adjusting to their loss.

As an author, she loves to pen down her thoughts and experiences to help people find their way through grief. Through her books, she wants to share her knowledge of how she survived the loss of her parent and loves to immerse herself in extensive research to provide valuable information that could benefit those most in need.

INTRODUCTION

" A mother's love is always with her children. Losing a mother is one of the deepest sorrows a heart can know. But her goodness, caring, and wisdom live on like a legacy of love that will always be with you. May that love surround you now bring you resilience, hope and comfort.

Several schools believe that a person's necessities include air, food, water, clothes, and shelter. However, we must also have "interactions and relationships" in this list because it might be difficult for a person to exist without close relationships with other people, places, and things. My personal story is a testimony to this. For someone growing up under the care and affection of her mother to suddenly lose not just those feelings of love but also the person from whom those feelings come can be devastating. It is always a difficult threshold to step over.

Let's begin with the months of pregnancy; during these months, a sometimes challenging but ultimately fulfilling relationship has already started. This is because mothers and their kids have some connections, even before childbirth. Due to their provision of fundamental needs such as food, drink, shelter, sleep, and the ability to establish a strong bond with their little child, mothers have a crucial impact on their offspring's mental well-being. The emotional connection that forms between a baby and a mother when cut short becomes an unbearable loss.

In most cases, the loss doesn't walk alone. It brings along its close accomplice: Grief. When we lose someone or something so dear to us, we experience intense, overpowering feelings that might be challenging to discuss. These feelings are known as "grief" in our contemporary society. But how can such nuanced emotions be expressed in a single word? That calls for us to explore the meaning and use of the word "grief".

Grief is the emotional reaction to loss, especially the loss of a person or other living object with whom you had a close attachment, affection and interaction. You might feel a wide range of challenging and unexpected feelings, such as bewilderment, remorse, fear, or extreme sadness. Loss's agonising pain might frequently seem unmanageable. Grief distress can also interfere with your physical well-being, making it challenging to do basic things like eating, sleeping, or even thinking clearly. These are common responses to loss; the greater the loss, the stronger your grieving will be.

It is believed that grief and "bereavement" are equivalent terms. Their meanings connect to the grieving process, even though they mean various things to different people. In contrast, some people see bereavement as a particular form of sadness when a loved one passes away. Others understand the term as the time frame when grief is experienced and losses are dealt with. Grief is a collection of agonisingly terrible feelings (it certainly feels that way most of the time). Each person goes through a different process of grieving, one that is as individual as their personality and connection to the loss. When grief is thoroughly understood, it can heal and evolve. It can, however, occasionally be a solitary process.

Grief is the process and feelings we go through when our significant relationships are abruptly ended or drastically disrupted. This could be due to death, divorce, movement, theft, damage, or another similar event. Although most people are familiar with the grief associated with death, people also experience grief in connection with various losses throughout their lives. This could include job loss, poor health, or the end of a romantic relationship.

A survey conducted in the US has it that; Grief strikes older people more frequently than younger people or children. Older folks often lose their spouses and friends, parents, and relatives. By 15, 1.5 million children (5 percent of all children in the US) are thought to have lost either or both parents. Also, each year, 2.5 million people pass away in the United States, resulting in 13 million grievers, leaving behind five mourners on average.

Another survey conducted among 1084 residents of the United States in 2019 stated that 780 of them had experienced loss due to a life event in the previous three years. One-third (31%) of people had experienced a significant sickness for themselves or a family member. Another third had experienced the death of a relative or close friend, and the final third had lamented the loss of similar relationships. Smaller percentages mourned divorce or other losses like lost employment, homes, or valuables.

From the statistics on loss and grief presented above, we can conclude that a sizeable portion of Americans experience grief every year.

Grief sets in when someone or something we care about passes away. In that grieving process, we mourn just those ties that have become important to us through time; we do not mourn all lost relationships. These relationships we regret can be a relationship with loved ones, spouses, significant others, friends, or other people with whom we share a close bond. Our relationships shape who we are and how we behave; they become deeply ingrained in our sense of self (or self-concept). As a result, they become an active component of who we are.

Losing one of these crucial relationships causes us to lose a significant portion of who we are, making it extremely painful. In actuality, grief and sadness are felt more strongly the more profound the loss is. Grief is not something that occurs "out there" in the world for this reason; instead, it takes place within each bereaved person's broken and individually wounded sense of self. The overwhelming array of feelings that the loss triggers gives rise to grief.

Regardless of whether someone's sadness is caused by the loss of a loved one or by receiving a terminal illness, grief is a powerful, perhaps overwhelming, feeling for people. They could have a sensation of numbness and disconnection from daily life, making it difficult for them to perform their regular tasks while dealing with their sense of loss. Grief has no predictable course. Everyone has their way of coping with sadness. While some say their grief lasts for weeks or months, others say it lasts years.

Also, everyone experiences grief differently, and it is a process or journey. It can be mentally and physically demanding, making it challenging to carry out routine tasks or leave the house. Some individuals turn to more activities and engagement to cope. Different feelings or behaviours may be experienced by people who are in grief. They could struggle with concentration, become reclusive, and not enjoy their typical hobbies. They may consume alcohol, tobacco, or drugs, utilise illicit substances, or harbour thoughts of harming themselves or giving up.

Grief can affect every aspect of one's life, including feelings, thoughts, behaviour, beliefs, physical health, sense of self and identity, and interpersonal connections. Feelings associated with a bereaved person include sadness, rage, anxiety, shock, regret, overwhelm, isolation, irritability, and numbness.

Just as it has been established previously, many people have, at one point in time or the other, had their share of grief experiences. You are not the first person. I lost my mom at a very tender age and had difficulty getting through that. Eventually, I saw the light at the end of the tunnel. From this experience, I have decided to help other individuals passing through a similar situation. I wish you an insightful read.

WE ALL HAVE A STORY

*I*n this chapter, you'll have access to stories about grief and loss, including mine. Nearly everyone has experienced grief due to the past loss of something or someone close to them. Some of those losses are worse and sound very much unbelievable. Stories have been put together from the accounts of courageous young people globally who shared their experiences with loss to support others who were going through a similar thing. Apart from the first story, which is my personal story, many things have been adjusted in the other stories, like the actual names of people and places, for confidentiality.

The fact that these people have sacrificed a portion of their lives to lessen suffering should inspire and brace you. This kind of expression can relieve some of your stress and help you feel less alone in your trying time.

ROSETTA'S STORY: MY PERSONAL STORY

Almost every child would say their mother is the best world; I would not say any other mother was better than mine. Mom had some qualities I assume to be superhuman, which stood her out among millions of other mothers worldwide. I've never been so close to anyone as I was with her. She was strong, versatile, and always carried a poker face, even amid adversities. We shared a connection that transcended a mother-to-child relationship. We were like sisters. I would relate to her like an elder sibling, and she would respond accordingly.

Growing up as a child, I used to get many people telling me how much my mom and I looked alike and how similar our smile was. I would always respond to these compliments with that same smile and, by doing so, get a feeling of my mom's presence even when we were distant apart. Mom was a woman of service and played active roles in the community by supporting local and national initiatives to empower women and provide a means of livelihood for them. She ran so many events at home to raise awareness and promote women's initiatives which she was very passionate about.

Everything went okay every day until we experienced the storm that would later separate us in this physical world in April 2005. During one of her planned events, where we had over 500 guests, her journey to the end started. While serving guests, she suddenly dropped, and her head significantly impacted the floor. She was rushed to the hospital, and multiple surgeries were carried out to the effect of the accident. Even with this series of surgeries, doctors could not relieve the pressure in her brain. It turned out that mom had a haemorrhage built from a lot of stress and anxiety in her brain.

My siblings and I didn't have so much time as the pressure was too much to contain. Around that period, I was at the college, wrapping up my degree as I was preparing for my final exams. I got a call that mom was in the hospital and under surgery. And before I could ever make it there, mom had taken her last breath, and there was no way to say good-bye. It was a challenging experience for me. The fact that I had lost someone so close at such a time was quite painful, and it was even more unfortunate that I couldn't get to say goodbye to her. Trust me, the period after the loss was not easy. I had passed through almost all the symptoms of grief, and I felt I would never be able to find my feet again. Well, I found my feet and learned to live with the loss, cherishing the memories of my mother and engraving them on the tablet of my heart.

LISTEN TO AVA TELL HER STORY

My mom and I had a tight relationship. I wouldn't know why the bond was so strong. Spending time with her was akin to spending time with an older version of me. We always preferred to occupy our time in the same manner. We enjoyed architecture, Greek cuisine, and musty used bookstores. We frequently wore the same dress since I always admired how she dressed.

When I was in primary school, she would occasionally take me out in the mornings to get steamed milk with vanilla for me and tea for herself. We would then sit in the cosiest chairs and read the newspaper. She would provide the comics to me while keeping the arts section to herself. These mornings were great. Most of our time together was spent watching game shows and shouting out the answers, even while she was ill. Spending time with her made me feel incredibly mature.

I learned that my mother was sick the summer following my first year of college. I had just turned 18 a few months earlier, and my mother had been diagnosed with breast cancer. We don't know exactly when she was ill because her breast cancer did not show any symptoms initially. She was feeling discomfort in the nipple area of her breast and a pulling in of the nipple. The doctors we took her to, a number of them struggled to identify the cause of her pain.

One day, my father received a call from the doctor recommending an oncologist; I was in that car that day with my dad. My dad took the recommendation and consulted with an oncologist. Shortly after, my mom received a stage 4 breast cancer diagnosis, which the doctor described as "the kind that you don't want to have." She has three years to live, they claimed.

She went through some surgeries a few months after being diagnosed. She eventually became someone who was no longer my mother due to chemotherapy, radiation, and other medications. In addition to being bald, frail, and underweight, she also had puffy cheeks from taking a steroid drug that caused her face to expand. She could not even wield a pen because of her severe neuropathy, which causes persistent pins and needles. She used an oxygen machine to breathe and moved with a walker. She would frequently say things that were illogical because of her foggy thinking. I kept wanting to call out, "Mom!" Come back!

In my second year of college, my mother passed away two days after returning home for spring break. She had been deteriorating steadily but didn't pass away until all her kids were home. Moms are rumoured to wait for all of their children, and it indeed appeared as my mom did.

A painful experience for me! The funeral was quite bizarre. The funeral marked the first time I had ever shed tears in front of anyone who wasn't my parents or sisters because I was emotionally guarded. I lost interest in everything and everyone, even after my mom had been buried. I felt like the whole world would fall on me.

SANDRA'S STORY

When Sandra's stepfather died when she was 17, she always referred to him as her father. She feared people wouldn't take her grief seriously if she stated he was her stepfather. Her father and best friend, Sandra's stepfather, lived with them and did everything with them. She knew that her stepfather and her mothers were soul mates and much in love. She stated that her stepfather served as the primary father figure in her youth because she did not have a solid relationship with her biological father. She heard her brother calling her name as he stood on their drive in September 2019 while she was making her way home from school. When she rushed to him, she discovered their stepfather huddled beneath their large off-road motorcycle. It had fallen on him when he was attempting to mend it. When she couldn't feel his pulse or check to see if he was breathing, she dialled 911 while her brother asked the neighbours to try and assist them. In the end, an air ambulance, fire trucks, and ambulances arrived to try to free him from the automobile. Sandra had to phone her mother's place of employment to explain what had happened. When she saw her mother yelling and crying as she got to the house, it destroyed her. Her mother had just suffered the loss of her beloved. Sandra's stepfather was eventually declared dead there and then. That was two weeks before her final in-person mock exam, ultimately used to determine her natural exam marks due to COVID. She did well in the exams, though. But she was aware that she had suppressed her feelings to focus on her studies, which was why she was only now beginning to absorb things.

Even though it has only been three years, her stepfather has already missed a lot. One of the hardest things for her is the realisation that she will never see him again and that they won't be able to share memories. She appears to be crying every day and thinks about him frequently. Sandra and her family haven't talked about his passing, but she is worried about her brother because she is aware of his struggles with suicidal ideas. Since they don't have a relationship where they can discuss their feelings, Sandra is unsure how to assist him. Both of them bottled it up, which was not helpful. She finds it uncomfortable to share her feelings with anyone. She hopes her stepdad keeps eyeing her because she misses him so much.

TASHA'S STORY

Tasha's parents were so close that you could call them soul mates. Her father met her mother when he was a grocery shop employee. Her mother and her friend went to purchase at her father's grocery shop. The following time she visited his shop, he offered her a love note that he had written, and she graciously accepted his invitation to go on a date. It turns out that when they lived next to one another, her dad would whistle underneath her building to let her know when they would meet. Through their windows, they would speak with one another. Despite all difficulties, they managed to have an intercaste marriage and were perfect for one another. They were continuously helping each other out.

Her father had smoked for thirty years. He made numerous attempts to quit, but his health got worse each time he did so. She was stunned when he died. Living without him was extremely difficult for her mother because she felt like a piece of her mother had died along with him. It was difficult for her to accept that he was no longer with them; she could not cry but knew she had to be vital to her mother. She continued texting and constantly talking about him days after he passed.

Later, as her mother recovered, they began spending all their free time together. Tasha's mother put a lot of effort into raising her as Tasha was going through a difficult period at school around this time. Boys were her only friends because they didn't engage in gossip. Without ever knowing her, the other females at school began calling her a "slut." Tasha never cursed at anyone since she was best at understanding that one can never truly understand what another person is going through. She started focusing her energies on photography, which allowed her to express herself and feel free.

Her attention and love were on her mother. They started taking frequent trips together. Tasha received a scooter from her mother for her 18th birthday! As usual, they travelled together on a highway when a collision occurred. Tasha was dozing off in the back seat of the car. She woke up and found blood all over her and surrounding her, but it wasn't her blood, so she had no idea what was happening. Her mother had suffered a severe head injury. Even though they were all on the road and requesting assistance, not a single car stopped for them.

Half of the passengers got out when a car finally stopped after an extended period. They drove Tasha's mother to the hospital. She had received a head injury and several fractures and didn't survive. She died.

At 20, Tasha was all by herself. She struggles to express how painful losing her mother was. Her mother was both a lifeline and her best friend.

She understood that she had obligations, including carrying food, handling money, and comprehending the value of money. For Tasha, it was a trying time. On her 16th birthday, her mother gave her a DSLR, and on her 18th, she got a scooter. According to her, It was intended to be a subtle hint from her mother that she should travel and do photography to pursue her passion.

KIKI'S STORY

Ten days before her 17th birthday, Kiki lost her younger brother to suicide.

One morning she woke up to her mother wondering if her brother, Freddie, was sleeping in her room. Her mother sprinted downstairs when he wasn't. When she got downstairs, her parents were in a panic since Freddie wasn't at home. Kiki was utterly perplexed by what had just occurred.

Freddie occasionally snuck out. She initially believed that he had gone to a friend's place. When she entered his room, she discovered a note addressed to her and her parents. She understood right away and instantly felt nauseous and miserable. When she gave her mother the letter, her mother was speaking with the police on the phone. When the cops showed up there, they demanded Kiki leave the room. She could hear her mother yelling. Near 1:00 am, they discovered Freddie's body at the base of a bridge above a road. Kiki was utterly stunned when her father revealed the news to her.

Kiki had a terrible time grieving; she wouldn't want it upon her greatest enemies. Since Kiki and her brother shared a separation of one year and ten months, they were practically best friends. She will never experience life as intended, and nothing will ever be the same for her. Although they have his ashes, it still doesn't feel natural to her. She hopes he is now in a far better situation, one in which he deserves to be, and has finally discovered contentment and happiness.

WE MIGHT WANT TO ASK: DOES EVERYONE GRIEVE THE SAME WAY?

Looking closely at these stories, we are near an answer to the above question.

Responses and reactions to grief come in a wide variety that is frequently perplexing.

Everyone experiences grief differently. When it doesn't live up to our demands, grieving can be one of the most challenging experiences. Instead of struggling to rise from bed, you might notice yourself being extremely busy. Alternatively, you might laugh throughout the burial rather than cry as you had anticipated. In these circumstances, we are frequently harshest on ourselves. We are adding the stress of having to meet our mental standards to everything else that accompanies grieving. Throughout the grieving process, it's crucial to allow yourself to take on whatever you can bear, including comprehending challenging queries about your feelings.

We experience grief and react to losses in various ways, for multiple causes and even for different lengths of time. There is no right or wrong way to grieve; it is a personal process. How people suffer is influenced by a variety of things, such as their personality and coping mechanisms, life experiences, religious beliefs, and the importance of the loss to them. There are other models for what grief might (or ought to) look like. Although The Stages of Grief are well recognised as a model for what takes place during the mourning process, there are other angles to consider. There are a few of them.

There's the Traumatic way of grieving. This traumatic reaction is the grief you experience after losing a parent suddenly or unexpectedly. For instance, perhaps you lost a parent or witnessed the horrific demise of a loved one. Traumatic grieving differs from the grief experienced after an anticipated loss, such as when a person dies after a protracted illness. This is not to say that they are less challenging to live with.

The tragic death of a parent and the accompanying grief are two burdens the suffering individual must bear. Your mind may be wondering things like, "Did they suffer? What did they last think? When they were dying, did they grieve for me? These might haunt you.

People who have suffered a devastating loss can have symptoms resembling PTSD. According to research on persons who had experienced a loss after the 9/11 attacks three years after the tragedy, roughly 43% of them were still experiencing symptoms of complicated grief combined with PTSD.

There's also the complicated way of grieving. The kind of grieving known as complicated grief gets worse with time. The term persistent complex bereavement disorder is frequently used to describe complicated grief. It is difficult to move past the loss and resume your own life when experiencing complicated grief since the painful emotions are so intense and long-lasting. It appears to begin as typical grief, but as time goes on, it deepens and becomes immobilised. This type of grief is incapacitating and frequently transformative. These excruciating grief-related pains don't get better with time. This kind of mourning is a mental health condition that can deepen depression and result in physical issues.

Furthermore, some grieve chronically. A grieving state known as chronic grief never gets better. You endure ongoing suffering and intense distress for a protracted period when you are in chronic mourning. Some people take their suffering for years on end without ever getting over their loss. If untreated, chronic grieving can lead to significant issues. The mourner's daily experience may likely include feelings of hopelessness, despair, anxiety, self-harm, suicidal thoughts, and others.

Grief can also be exaggerated. It is an intensification or magnifying of the typical grief process. Exaggerated grieving will initially manifest as common grief, which will intensify over time. Suicidal thoughts, anger, self-mutilation, and other self-destructive behaviours are just a few ways this sort of grieving might appear.

But how can one tell if the grieving is not just "regular"? How can you know when the grief has become overdone, and the feelings are out of control? Exaggerated grieving is a subset of complicated grief, including other types. The griever typically experiences deep feelings that endure for three to six months before gradually waning as time passes and acceptance sets in. This escalation worsens as time passes, making life more challenging and grieving overwhelming. However, even after three to six months, for a griever who takes their grief too far (exaggerate), it only worsens—most times—magnified grief results from the fact that the bereaved do not want to come out of their grief and move on. It's an intentional kind of grief.

On a general ground, a person who has recently lost a parent might frequently have hallucinations, dreams in which the deceased is still alive, "sees" the dead in public, and other delusions and misconceptions. However, these actions become less frequent, and sorrow creeps in when the missing person does not show up. Then, it's typical to have symptoms like intense melancholy, low moods, trouble concentrating, rage, guilt, impatience, anxiety, and restlessness. Due to the bereaved person's attention being on the deceased, offers of comfort and assistance are frequently declined. Additionally, typical are crying and general tearfulness. The suffering may lose interest in the outer world at this time and often stop doing things they used to love, such as eating, watching television, or socialising.

As noted above, potentially unhealthy behaviours, such as smoking and drinking, may worsen after a loss, particularly in those who had a propensity for doing so before the flop. Because they frequently occur in bereaved people, these actions may be typical. However, they are also physically and mentally destructive of themselves, possibly causing cirrhosis of the liver and lung cancer. Substance addiction and other risky behaviours, including irresponsible driving, may not seem like overt attempts at suicide, but they can accomplish the same thing.

The emotions of the bereaved may change abruptly and quickly from one feeling state to another, and for a while, avoiding thoughts of the departed may be alternated with purposeful memory-building. People typically transition from scepticism to progressive acceptance of the loss's reality. The bereaved may have understood the loss' finality mentally before their emotions allowed them to accept the new knowledge as accurate. Although no two suffering people are precisely the same, most people experience depression and emotional swings for at least a few months and frequently for more than a year after losing a loved one.

ANTICIPATORY GRIEF: THERE'S ALWAYS A TIME BEFORE THE STORM

There is time and season for everything in life, whether good or bad. Most of us believe that the grieving season occurs after the storm of life has struck one so hard. Well, I wouldn't say this is true because there's also a time before the storm: even though it is yet to arrive, one is undoubtedly expecting it. Grieving can begin long before a person passes away, but this is frequently not accepted, spoken of, or even recognised.

If you know that an individual is likely to pass away soon, it's pretty normal to start grieving before that person's death. Grief, for example, can begin as soon as a loved one is given a terminal prognosis. These emotions and moods can all be just as solid and challenging as those that follow a death. This emotion is referred to as anticipatory grief since it happens before the actual end or other loss, such as losing one's capabilities or freedom. A patient who is down with an illness or dying and their dear ones can suffer anticipatory grief.

Forbes Health (2022) refers to anticipatory grief as some despair an individual may experience in the weeks, months, or even years preceding the loss of a beloved one or another imminent bereavement. Grief of this kind can be experienced on various planes, including the mental, bodily, interpersonal, and spiritual.

There is no standard measure of grief that someone will experience with every grieving reaction, and having anticipatory grief just before a parent passes away does not guarantee that the subsequent grief will be any less intense. Every bond is as distinct as the people in it, so your mourning will invariably be specific to that special connection.

When a parent passes away abruptly, you do not have the opportunity to bid farewell. Even yet, grieving before death does not take the place of, or even decrease, the time spent grieving after death. You could think it's inappropriate to communicate the intense agony you're experiencing because this type of grief isn't frequently spoken about in society. The assistance you need might not be provided as a result.

WHAT DISTINGUISHES ANTICIPATORY GRIEF FROM OTHER TYPES OF GRIEF?

Although anticipatory grief may not seem different from grieving after someone passes away, the significant distinction is that anticipatory grief takes place before the loss happens. Some particular difficulties arise when mourning a parent who is still alive.

First of all, anticipating grieving is not universal. For some people, it might be a very effective coping mechanism to deny what is beginning to happen, and grieving might be seen as losing hope.

Living knowing that a loved one will soon pass away can leave some people feeling torn. While they struggle with the thought of losing their beloved ones if they eventually pass away, people tend to simultaneously cling to the hope that they won't lose them, with the hope that maybe some miracle might still happen. They might oscillate back and forth between these two extremes. It is sensitive and challenging to deal with this circumstance. You can start to let go while still clinging to hope.

This is painful to some individuals. If they have the slightest tendency toward releasing off, they could feel betrayed by their loved ones. The fact is that it is possible to hang on to something while also letting go of it. No decision is required of you.

These feelings might cause excruciating discomfort. Even worse, it's harder for individuals to find help during this period for their loss. Other folks who haven't gone through this situation before occasionally have adverse reactions. They might believe that you have given up on the dying individual.

Anticipatory grief may have more to do with your present way of life than with the sick parent. This is particularly valid if you devote much energy to caring for them. You could miss doing things you liked to do together and be sad about how your bond has changed.

When you start acting as a caregiver or when you begin receiving care, the structure of your interaction could shift. Adjusting to and accepting these shifts may require some time. It's crucial to keep in mind that grieving before a loss can cause intense, debilitating emotions. Still, there is assistance ready to help you manage.

Although it is prevalent, however, not everyone experiences anticipatory grief. While your dear one is still alive, experiencing grief does not signify that you are losing hope in them or even leaving them with their lot. Instead, anticipating grief may present an opportunity for you to find a purpose and resolution that you might not have. One that might carry you through if the loss eventually happens.

DIFFERENT STAGES OF ANTICIPATORY GRIEF

Just like normal or conventional grief, anticipatory grief also has different stages that are unique to it. Using the anticipatory grief of losing a parent as a case study, each of the following steps may occur in many instances, degrees, and orders during the display of grief:

Stage 1: At this point, the individual accepts that death is unavoidable and has no hope for recovery. Despair and sorrow frequently accompany this initial stage.

Stage 2: The worry for the dying individual is the following stage. Close relatives could regret arguing with the dying parent or reprimanding them. The dying parent may become more worried about themselves and their mortality anxieties. The parent might be concerned about the feelings their loved ones, particularly their children, are expressing.

Stage 3: The actual death may be "rehearsed" during this stage. In this stage, worries include the real death experience and potential afterlife scenarios. Some anticipatory grief may lead to making burial plans and bidding farewell to loved ones.

Stage 4: During the final stage, family members can picture their lives without the departing individual. Dying parents can be considering the items they would leave behind, anniversaries and birthday celebrations for kids they would miss, or even who would cover for their kids in the areas where they have always functioned. What it will look like to lose a parent is something that children might question. The dying individual might contemplate life after death. They might also make an effort to envision it.

ANTICIPATORY GRIEF COMES WITH SIGNS AND SYMPTOMS

The signs that come with anticipatory grief are comparable to those that follow a loss. You need to understand them first before you can start to think about a coping mechanism. They might even sometimes resemble a roller coaster. There could be tough days. You might not experience any grief on other days as everybody grieves in unique ways. However, the following signs are popular among people experiencing anticipatory grief:

*S*orrow **and separation anxiety:** Sorrow and separation anxiety tend to increase quickly and frequently appear when least expected. An unexpected and heartbreaking signal that your loved one is passing away could come from anything as common as a television ad. The sudden wave of worry may be just as strong as when you initially discovered that the same person dear to your heart was dying.

Separation anxiety is more familiar with children expecting the death of their mother since there's a special bond between mothers and their kids. The anticipation of living without someone so dear to one's heart causes the sorrow and pain accompanying anticipatory grieving. That feeling might be accompanied by a sizeable quantity of worry and anxiety. You can be afraid that your habits might be altered, your social lifestyle might be lost, or you might become lonely without your mom. These sentiments are not exclusive to relatives and friends. Even though it is a sort of anticipatory sadness, the dying person could feel anxious and lonely. All through the course of the illness, this grief is felt both physically and mentally.

Fear: Fear is a universal experience when it comes to anticipatory grief. In addition to what death would eventually bring itself, you can be afraid of the adjustments that will come with losing that person you hold dear to your heart. A loved one's death can cause unimaginable fear. The emotions that arise in you when a loved one is diagnosed with a terminal illness can seem impossible and terrible. Due to the Covid-19 pandemic, hundreds of households have had to find a way to deal with the possibility of losing a loved one. Consequently, there is an increase in the number of people feeling afraid and sad about impending death.

Realising death is inevitable, and circumstances can be beyond your reach is one thing; experiencing mental calm due to this realisation is quite another. Expecting yourself to be calm and collected is unrealistic. After all, you can anticipate the passing of a loved one. Allow yourself to experience fear and sorrow.

If any of the following situations apply to you, watch out for natural apprehension and grief that could develop into an undesirable condition of immobility or distraction for your benefit and that of your dear one :

- Incapable of providing for basic needs
- Unable to take care of yourself properly, or
- Too absorbed with memories of your loved one's passing to appreciate the present moment fully

*G*uilt: Many people experience severe guilt before a loved one's passing. For example, you might want the person's pain to cease, which may also result in death. Having "survivor guilt" is a common reaction to knowing that your existence will continue even after they are gone. Additionally, you can feel guilty about previous actions or disputes between you and the ailing person. You could also feel guilty for being able to enjoy things they cannot want due to their present circumstances.

Few emotions underlying guilt are more challenging to understand. A person could have guilt after feeling comforted that their dying relative would no longer suffer if they passed away. That's from comfort to blame. Someone may experience fury about uncontrollable events that have led to the approaching death and then become guilty for their anger. That's from rage to regret. The emotion that frequently goes along with other grief-related sentiments is guilt. One of the reasons it is so challenging to comprehend is because of this.

*A*nger and frustration: While it is true that people looking after a sick loved one might feel angry, especially toward themselves, the feeling of anger is more common among the dying individual. Anger is a typical response to a severe loss. A dying person risks losing everything and everyone that matters to them. Their condition could make them feel cheated. If they believe in a supernatural influence, they might accuse God of causing or failing to heal the disease. They could even resent their loved ones for carrying on with their lives as they steadily lose theirs. They might believe that their physician isn't being honest with them, that their caregivers aren't accommodating to their requests, and that the universe has already begun to abandon them.

Individuals may also feel angry when a loved one is dying. Angry at feeling neglected. Angry that our lives would be changed, angry that handling our grief feels challenging, and mad that the earth feels completely bad, dangerous, or helpless.

Feelings that are buried don't go away. Alternatively, they could catalyse unaddressed grief, melancholy, stress, or even persistent medical problems. Allowing your emotions, no matter what they may be, is crucial to overcoming grief. Anger is not usually accepted in our culture. However, anger is a normal emotion that is not harmful; it is only an emotion like any other. However, most people still struggle with seeing anger as a normal emotion everyone experiences.

. . .

*L*oss of self: People caring for a dying loved one may give up their everyday lives during this dedicated stage of caring. They prioritise the loved one's needs over their own. They lose their friends, hobbies, and routines. And they ignore their own psychological or physiological demands. Some people grow numb to help them better handle the dying process. People looking after a dying loved one may be under constant stress, become easily agitated, and feel compelled to run away from their obligations. They might live a chaotic life themselves.

A person watching their loved one dying could simultaneously feel helpless, nervous, worried, depressed, and resentful. Such people may endure a lot of physical difficulties. They can oversleep or have trouble falling asleep. They might eat too much or not, resulting in drastic weight loss or growth. Dizziness, a lack of focus, and discomfort accompany tiredness and fatigue. Individuals may lose enthusiasm for items or hobbies that once gave them joy. People mourning ahead of time for a dying soul could feel as though they have no one to turn to for assistance or that there is no way to express their feelings, which would further isolate them from colleagues and relatives.

WHY ANTICIPATORY GRIEF COULD BE SUITABLE FOR PREPARATION FOR LOSS

When a loved one passes away suddenly, many individuals wish they had a long time to get used to the possibility of living without them. We have an opportunity to comprehend and come to terms with this person's impending passing through anticipatory grieving.

Anticipatory grief offers persons who are dying a chance for growth at the end of their lives. It might be a means to get resolution and significance. Families can use this time to resolve conflicts, forgive one another, and come to terms with the past. The opportunity to say farewell can seem like a gift to both parties. You open up chances to mend broken relationships or make statements you've always wanted to make, such as "I love you" and "I'm sorry if I've been mean to you." Thus expressing your sorrow healthily.

Anticipatory grief can be used as a dynamic warm-up for future events. And be taught to value the moment you still get to be alongside your cherished one.

Families will occasionally skip seeing a loved one who is passing away. They might come up with the following reasons: "I am not sure I can bear the pain of visiting," or "I do not want to have the memory of my loved one with that emaciated body." In this situation, anticipating grief can be therapeutic.

DEALING WITH ANTICIPATORY GRIEF

Even while anticipating grief is natural, it may negatively impact your well-being as a whole. Allow yourself to experience the anguish of grief without fear. There is no remedy for repressing or ignoring these emotions. Recognise your sentiments of loss and anxiety and tell yourself they are typical for your circumstances. Here are some strategies to help control anticipatory grieving if you're having difficulties processing your emotions or understanding them:

*R*ecognise that grieving ahead of time is natural. You are okay, and it's acceptable to feel sad before a loss. You have the right to experience this kind of sorrow. You're not the first to ever have this feeling, and you wouldn't be the last! It has been known for almost a generation that this is a typical occurrence.

*A*ccept your losses. It might be upsetting when people trivialise your situation by saying, "At least your parent is still alive." Recognise that even though the individual hasn't passed away, you are still mourning for them. If you're having trouble expressing your feelings about accepting your impending loss, losing hope, losing a loved one, losing the future you envisioned, etc., think about writing, arts, photography, or other artistic avenues. Investigate meditation as a method of being awake and conscious of the numerous feelings you are managing.

Get connected to people that can help. People looking after a dying individual frequently experience anticipatory grief. Still, when caregiving takes up all of your attention, it's possible to feel lonely and alienated. Look for local or online caregiver support networks so you may interact with people who can relate to your struggles, such as anticipatory grieving. Keep in touch with the outside world. Although it may be tempting to withdraw, engaging in routine activities might help you feel "okay" even when what you're living through may seem to be starving you of it.

You shouldn't give up if you experience anticipatory grief; keep that in mind. You are not abandoning a close relative as much as you are there to assist. We frequently conclude that a condition is irreversible and that complete recovery is no longer possible at some point. Even though it is a fact, accepting it may leave you with a guilty sense. Concentrate on what you are doing, such as continuing to support, love, care for, and spend quality time with each other. Your focus is changing from your desire for complete healing to your passion for quality time spent together.

*T*hink about the time you have left. Think of how you and your dying relative would like to interact during that time. Even though our wishes aren't always realised, try your best to make the most of the time you have left with your beloved relative or parent in a manner that both of you feel fulfilling. To confirm that you can respect your loved one's desires, you might want to talk about real issues like leaving a will behind and burial preparations if they are receptive to it, instead of being forced to speculate on what they would have preferred.

*B*e open to discussion. Everybody experiences anticipatory grieving diversely, just as we all grieve in diverse ways. Be aware that various family members may encounter and deal with anticipatory grieving in myriad ways. Maintaining open discussion can improve everyone's understanding of one another. Make sure to involve all the significant people among your relatives and close associates in those discussions if you want the time you have left to be enjoyable and worthwhile. Maintaining open lines of communication is crucial while experiencing anticipatory grief. It could be challenging for you to discuss your loved one's illness and potential demise with them. Using humour can be beneficial in this case. Still, you must pay attention to the person's emotional state if the intent is not received correctly.

Take mothers, for instance; you wouldn't understand that your mother had left with vast knowledge until a few days after she passed away. Who do you contact if you have inquiries regarding your family, meals, history, or general living? You give your mother a call. Severing this connection means severing ties to your past. Make a list of inquiries and note the responses, as this is the narrative of your family. Note it down while you can.

*L*ook after your well-being. Keep in mind the adage that you cannot look after the well-being of others if you do not look after yours first. Taking care of your health and welfare when caring for or anticipating the loss of a loved one with a terminal illness is crucial to have the stamina and fortitude needed for your caregiver duties. It can be simple to place your concerns last. Still, it's vital to take care of yourself if you're feeling worn out or exhausted so you can continue to provide support for the person who requires it the most. You must continue engaging in your favourite hobbies outside of your care-giving job. Taking pauses from providing care consistently will prevent you from being stressed out. You can have the stamina you need for your work as a caregiver by feeding and resting well, unwinding, engaging in physical activity, and caring for your general well-being.

*A*ccept counselling if offered! I know that a few of us may still believe that counselling may be unnecessary, but this is untrue. Counselling might be helpful for regular, average individuals who need a space to process complicated feelings and get some alone space. Accept counselling if offered to avoid becoming overpowered by feelings of impending sadness.

*I*t is natural to feel relieved. When losses are predicted, there may be weeks, months, or years of caring that can be daunting and draining. It's pretty natural to feel relief when someone passes away. Yet, this sensation can also leave you feeling guilty. Having comfort after a loss you predicted does not indicate you cherished the individual any less; keep that in mind. After going through a difficult and unpleasant period in your life, this is a natural feeling.

. . .

*N*ever make assumptions. Everyone experiences grief in different ways. Do not presume that your loss was foreseen; your grieving would progress more slowly or quickly following the death.

When dealing with anticipatory grief, you must start by acknowledging your emotions; all the feelings we have listed earlier are pretty standard. You don't need to feel guilty for any of these emotions because you're a good person for experiencing such emotions. Recognise that some periods will be more brutal to get through than others. There may be waves of grief. The tide may flow in and then leave again. Take a break from sorrow for a while. It is unnecessary to worry about and care for your loved one constantly. Use hubbies or anything you adore doing about yourself to divert your attention.

RELATING WITH A DYING SOUL

*I*t's only normal to think about utterances to make and actions to consider when you find that a good friend or a close relative has been given a diagnosis with a terminal illness. It's normal to experience feelings of helplessness or inadequateness. You can still contribute positively if your loved one enters their last moments. You must show consideration for a friend or relative's emotional needs. Everybody has various requirements. While some value "usual" conversation and connections, those experiencing painful emotions may require chances to express themselves.

People frequently experience anxiety and dread when contemplating death. Our death becomes quite evident when we consider the deaths of others. Individuals dying could feel distant or alone from loved ones and companions struggling with this phase. This makes it understandable why many terminally ill individuals express being alone. Most of us might not choose this way of dying, for sure. Most of us would like to spend our final weeks or days with friends and family. Finding the right words of comfort for a loved one who is dying can be difficult and painful. Your thoughts are daily, regardless of whether you are under pressure to say the proper thing or unsure where to start.

WHY DO PEOPLE FIND IT HARD TO RELATE TO A DYING SOUL?

The fact that many people find it hard to relate to someone dying can be attributed to several factors, including a lack of emotional stamina, a desire to avoid facing their mortality, and insufficient time. An individual may avoid a terminally ill person out of regret thinking they could have taken maybe a step or two to stop the illness, or because of how they have lately interacted with that individual.

Avoidance, trouble communicating, difficulty establishing eye contact, and keeping a physical space are common signs that someone is finding it hard to relate with a terminally ill individual or parent. These symptoms are likely to be noticed by the dying person. Everyone passes away differently, so depending on how much pain or other painful symptoms they are experiencing and how they handle it, the dying individual may cause more significant avoidance. Some dying persons might not want to have lengthy chats but enjoy quick, direct interaction. These issues may make loved ones feel worse than they already do.

However, putting the following into consideration could help you better in relating to a dying person:

1. You should show concern

It is beneficial to let your relative or ailing friend realise that you bear them at heart and are worried about their health. However, there must be a balance between showing just enough care and going overboard with it. The difference between asking, "What are the chances you're going to survive it?" and simply stating, "This must be very terrible for you" or "In what way can I help or assist you?". This encourages unwanted contemplation on the sickness, with the latter stemming from great concern to assist the ailing individual.

Three words can sometimes be all it requires to soothe people the most. For example, "I love you." Remember to manifest your concerns during these difficult times. Let them realise they are loved and cherished regardless of how you prefer to communicate your affection through words, pictures, flowers, or writing. There isn't a right or simple method to handle these situations or exchanges. Above all, try to maintain your genuineness while being encouraging and compassionate. Remember that it's acceptable to admit while speaking with a dying friend or relative that you do not possess all the responses. Weep, convey your feelings honestly, and stay quiet; at times, the right words are those that are not said.

People tending to a dying soul are always their closest friends or relative. Consequently, they frequently experience their loved one's despair and anxieties firsthand. Relating to such feelings, you must guarantee that the patient won't be left behind. You should ensure you give the dying soul stability so they can examine their mental hopes and miseries and accept their death. Also, you should reassure your loved one that their soul is cherished and that they are appreciated. You must fight with your loved ones the enormous dread, despair, and sorrow as they approach their impending death. It would help if you were intimately involved in observing and repressing the dying soul's anxiety, worry, and pain.

Due to the difficulties they face on their own, people going through the dying process frequently lash out in fury at their friends or relatives. Such dying loved ones could feel helpless, ignored, or unimportant even to their closest folks. They frequently vent their rage on someone close just because that individual is pretty close. Relating to such, you must control your rage and work to provide the loved one with as much assistance as you can. By showing much concern, you can assist the sick patient in identifying the causes of their rage and finding more effective ways to communicate their displeasure. The loved one must be reassured by you that their wants and anxieties are being taken into account and that the disease is not a "prison sentence." To achieve this, you must forgo your sentiments to prioritise the needs of the dying loved one. This is just one of the psychological sacrifices you must offer to ensure a smooth transition of the dying soul.

The individual who is dying might also have particular worries and apprehensions. They can be worried or fearful of the future or the people left behind. Some folks are concerned about dying in solitude. The responses of relatives, colleagues, and hospital staff might exacerbate these emotions. For instance, relatives and friends might stop coming since they don't know what to do to support or say, or they might pull back as they might already be mourning the dying person. As they cannot provide additional care, doctors attending to dying patients too may feel powerless and steer clear of patients in the end. This is why it is imperative to show utmost concern for the dying soul.

Chat with the individual to see if they can understand you. Chat about the topics you have always discussed, such as life, local happenings, and each other's hobbies and passions. Look over any picture they might have, or bring some of your own to share.

Give your loved one a book to read if the individual enjoys a specific title or author. You could also take on reading if the person cannot do so. Suppose you sense the person is unable to talk. In that case, you could only ask questions, demanding yes or no responses, enabling the individual to nod. A lengthy story could occasionally be complex for the individual to grasp or understand. Maybe read a single page or shorter fiction if that is the situation. Consider reading some hilarious stories; many individuals enjoy comedy.

Additionally, you could read aloud scripture verses, devotions, rhymes, magazines, or maybe something else the individual enjoys.

Another excellent alternative is to play songs and sing along to the person's favourite tunes. Trust me; even if your voice isn't perfect, it will look as though it is ideal to the parent, and you will later remember those enjoyable moments. Conversing about the day, contemporary affairs, histories, etc., is delightful for other people. Talk about your joint activities. "Recall when we..." Discuss your shared recollections while laughing. Ask the individual about their childhood, upbringing, education, employment, wedding, and relatives, such as brothers, fathers, elders, etc., if you don't know much about their background.

Touch is significant to the majority of individuals. Obtain consent first to grasp your beloved one's hand, brush their hair, or apply moisturiser to their body. They might find that uncomfortable or just be opposed to being touched. If you feel at ease doing so, say reassuring words like "I love you, "as I have said earlier, then offer an embrace and let the individual know how much you will miss them.

Be empathic to the sick, your family, friends, and everyone else in your vicinity. At this period, anxieties might be very high. An old wound may reopen. Siblings may fight and will fight. Remember that everybody experiences anxiety, sorrow, and grief in a diverse way and that you are all in this together. What is ideal for you may not be suitable for those around you. Maintain your focus on virtue. Do not forget to hug and bid farewell. Although it could be challenging, the dying person and you are aware of the impending death. If the other person is willing, bid them farewell. It's acceptable if there are tears and sorrow present.

2. Provide emotional and spiritual support

Relating well with a dying soul would help such a dying relative or loved one cope with their emotional and psychological needs. It makes sense that someone conscious and near death might experience depression or anxiety. Treatment for mental distress and grief is crucial. To promote dialogues about emotions, you might wish to get in touch with a therapist; perhaps one experienced with dying-related issues. If the distress is severe, medication might be helpful.

Some individuals may exhibit bizarre or abnormal behaviour and suffer emotional confusion, making communicating with their loved ones challenging. We discussed many ways to get out of the emotional chaos in the previous section, which talks about showing concern. These include bodily contact, engaging the dying person in communication, and helping them with stability. One thing that could be added to these is being present. This could make a person who is dying feel even less alone.

That you're available, live and direct, flesh and blood, is what it means to be present. This moment with your loved one doesn't necessarily need to be filled with conversation or care for their everyday needs. Simply being aware of your presence can make them feel cherished and welcomed for who they are. Then, there could be a mental shift from this singular act. Based on the circumstance, you may wish to hang out, talk about daily occurrences, or see a great movie while still around one another. Ensuring the parent feels loved and valued can be done by being around. If they can speak, pay close attention to what they're going to say without considering your following action. The ultimate present you can give to someone dying can be your company.

The spiritual demands of those nearing death may be just as significant as their physical demands. Finding purpose in life, resolving interpersonal conflicts, or coming to terms with one's situation are all examples of spiritual needs. A dying individual could find solace in addressing unresolved conflicts with friends or relatives. A therapist or counsellor's sessions could be beneficial. Many individuals find comfort in their beliefs. Others could experience difficulties with their spirituality or religion. Meditating, studying religious literature, or listening to spiritual songs could be helpful. A pastor, imam, monk, or rabbi are examples of members of religious groups the ailing individual can speak with.

Family members and friends might discuss the value of their bonds with the ailing individual. Grown kids, for instance, might discuss how their father has shaped their career path. Grandchildren should express to their grandfather how much he means to them. Friends can talk about the worth of decades of friendship and getting each other's back. Suppose relatives and associates cannot be there in person. In that case, they can submit recorded audio or video capturing their testimonies or maybe write a letter that would subsequently be read aloud.

Another way some individuals find calm as they approach death is by exchanging happy memories. Everybody can find consolation in this. Some medical professionals believe that even when a patient is unconscious, they can always hear. Let's take the unconscious stage, for example. In a 2020 article, Harbour Light Hospice established that people are out and unable to react to any stimuli when they are in a coma; however, the mind might be able to detect sounds from friends and family. Research indicates that communicating with and cuddling a loved one while unconscious may aid recovery. Introduce yourself to the individual as soon as you enter the room. Here, you don't have to speak about the dying person; instead, converse with them directly, even when it seems they cannot hear. It can be a good idea to ask somebody to record several of the remarks made during this period, the ones you made and the ones the ailing individual made. In the future, relatives may find solace in these recordings.

A mentally unbalanced dying individual could experience a moment when they appear to be reasoning. Profit from these opportunities while keeping in mind that they are probably transitory and not always an indication of things improving. A dying person can occasionally see or communicate with those who are not present. Sounds unbelievable, right? It's true. We've seen and heard of so many related near-death experiences. Those things are at the spiritual level; at this point, avoid the need to rebuke them, interfere in what they are saying, or imply that they are hallucinating things. Allow the dying soul to explore their world in peace. Sometimes those near death will report experiencing visions in which they meet departed family members, close associates, or some religious leaders. Such reflections may elicit various responses from the dying individual, but they are frequently highly consoling to them.

Irrespective of whether your loved one is merely spiritual or a devoted follower of their religion, they could be unsure and anxious about what will happen next. They could be reluctant to start discussions regarding their ideas. Watch for cues that they want to talk about these things, and pay attention to any opportunities they may provide you. Regardless if it comes from you or you volunteer to invite a preacher to converse with them, they might find consolation in knowing that a supernatural force exists and that eternity is possible.

3. Assist with practical activities

Numerous people strive to offer support in the most critical areas while a loved one is struggling with the process of death. Strangely enough, those who are dying might worry more about how things will get done without them. Often, this is the area where you can help the most. You could foresee several stressors as a loved one starts the journey of passing away. Putting aside the psychological, emotional, social, and religious problems that the dying might encounter, navigating daily life may present the most significant amount of confusion. One of the most critical sources of relief people may meet during the process of death is the knowledge that everything will be handled appropriately after their departure. An enormous amount of assistance can be given in this situation by you as a friend or relative of the dying person.

Some of the most critical questions asked by a person barely clinging to life are also the most straightforward. Examples include: "Who will water my garden?" "Who will care for my hubby?" "Who will give my dog food?" "Who is going to pick the kids up from school?" "Who will prepare breakfast for my family?" Even if you're probably not the health expert making important decisions regarding the deathbed or palliative care for your loved one, you can still make a big difference by handling the daily responsibilities that the dying person used to manage.

Someone dying could be concerned about how matters will be handled when they pass away. As life gradually comes to a halt, many practical activities need to be completed to help the one clinging to life at their final moment and the relative or friend taking care of such a person. Reassuring statements from a relative or friend, such as "I'll see to it that your garden is looked after," "Claire has agreed to take care of your dog," or "Mom, do not worry, I am going to take excellent care of my siblings," may assist in bringing about some amount of calm. You might say something to the effect that their matters are in capable hands.

You undoubtedly want to take something that will directly benefit your loved one and produce results. Offer to assist her with daily activities. Take her to routine checkups, clean her home, and do her chores. She will be grateful for the assistance and will realise that you value her enough to make time in your hectic routine to assist her. In some instances, aiding and supporting the dying individual's household is even more crucial. This assistance is frequently provided by setting up meal deliveries, collecting groceries, taking care of postal service, and attending to other everyday needs that might become exhausting or challenging.

While doing this, you should accept help in case anyone is offering to give a helping hand. You should not be obligated to manage your loved ones' bodily and mental demands on top of your frequent commitments if you are the sole caregiver for one who is passing. Additional people from the family, colleagues, and neighbourhood will likely offer their assistance. While you might think their help will burden them, remember that you are relieving their concerns about your current situation by giving them a few of the daily duties. They get bothered about your ability to perform all the everyday work while offering the necessary psychological assistance. This is the reason they would offer their support. You assist both yourself and them by allowing them to help you.

4. Learn to cope and be receptive

Learning to cope with and being receptive toward your dying loved one is directly proportional to relating with a dying person. After you have extended a gesture of concern and love and given all the support and assistance (emotional, spiritual and physical), you must now learn to cope with any tantrum a dying person might throw. Chief among many things you have to cope with in this situation is anger and frustration coming from the dying loved one. It is funny that they might be angry at you for even being too caring and supportive; they might get mad and frustrated at anything.

When adjusting to impending death, people frequently go through expected phases. Confusion, anger, pleading, sadness, and acceptance are a few of these. Most individuals dying will go through a stage of anger and frustration, albeit not all do and not usually in that sequence. But just in case, you must develop a coping mechanism to effectively relate with the dying person and make their journey to the netherworld easy and smooth. It makes sense that your loved one would be angry with you because anger can be readily transferred to other people. Peradventure, you find yourself and your loved one in such a situation; the first thing to do is to relate to them like a grown-up, even when they act like kids.

This is my reason for saying that: It's common practice to handle a sick individual like a kid because doing so is in line with human behaviour. You feel because they are incapacitated, you can order them around. If you find yourself in this cycle, that is, a relationship that used to be between two grown-ups now suddenly turns into "a grown-up ordering a kid around" one, and the dying loved one is likely to become even angrier, which will only have the opposite effect. You might not even be aware that you've adopted this behavioural habit. As a result, you'll probably encounter hostility from others. As a terminally sick person, losing your freedom and privacy is upsetting and embarrassing enough without getting handled like a kid. Accept it or not, a dying person wishes to maintain authority over their life, body, and choices. It's crucial to provide the dying loved ones with the freedom to convey their thoughts, determine their own decisions, and maintain their independence as much as possible to get over their anger.

Another way to relate well to a dying person's anger and frustration is to not take anything personally from them. Sometimes, those who are upset look for somebody else to blame. It's challenging to avoid taking offence when someone is angry at you and wondering, "Where did I get it wrong?" It's critical to remember that the person dying is not furious with you; instead, it's with their disease and circumstance as a whole. Even though they may be angry with you, it is not because of your wrongdoing.

You should also try and see life from their perspective. Just put yourself in their shoes. Although it's hard to understand entirely how some other individuals feel, attempting to comprehend issues from their perspective might help you better learn why they behave in a particular way. Think about being robbed of everything life offers you and consider the ailing individual's life: all the people they cherish, the things they like doing, the job accomplished, and the ambitions they have towards the future. From this perspective, it makes sense why they are upset. They risk losing everything they care about and all they have ever valued. Remember that worry about the future or potential bodily pain is frequently the primary source of anger. To confront and possibly alleviate some of these worries, it is vital to pay close attention to them and to encourage a loved one to talk about them with their healthcare professional.

Get angry at the ailment rather than the person it afflicted to understand the dying soul better. You can comprehend that a dying loved one's anger is justifiable if you fully grasp the origin of their anger. Your loved ones can manage their emotions by channelling their anger toward their disease.

Being enraged at the actual offender of the dying person could be beneficial. Feel free to be angry at the sickness.

𝒲rapping Up

Even though losing a person you love is difficult, you may still enjoy most of your remaining time around each other. Create fun experiences while spending a moment with the people you care about. Avoid dwelling on despair and regret and saying things such as "I only wished I had devoted more time to our relationship." You would only be wasting time to do better things while dwelling on things you can't even help. An essential point is simply being with the dying person because you never know when and how that moment will come again. Death is inevitable.

LOSING A MOTHER AS A TEENAGER

*a*fter the whole period of anticipation comes the actual loss. Though we grieve while a loved one is dying, we might eventually grieve more after they have passed away. This is regardless of how prepared we seem while anticipating imminent death. Though it often happens so fast, the whole process of dying might seem like a dream or some kind of fiction movie, especially if we are witnessing it for the first time. We might ask ourselves rhetorical questions like: "Is this how people die?" "So, mom is gone just like that?"

WHAT HAPPENS DURING THE DYING PROCESS?

Dying happens in stages. It entails the end of human bodily, mental, interpersonal, and spiritual life. As mortals, we don't know what transpires after death, whether there's an after-life or not. According to MILNE Library, the dying process is the sequence of activities that often occur before someone dies. The change an individual passes through before passing away is known as the process of dying. The manner of death and how each individual goes through it are personal. Every person has a unique experience with death, and everyone passes away at their own pace.

MILNE Library explains two common paths to transition during dying: the easy and rugged paths. The best we can aspire for while providing care for people near the end of their lives is the easy path. Sedation and drowsiness are the first symptoms, followed by the stage of the unconscious and, eventually, death. The thorny path starts with agitation and bewilderment and frequently leads to nasty hallucinations and dementia. And the dying person may experience physical indications and symptoms either months, weeks, days, or even hours before passing away. These symptom manifestations can also differ from individual to individual. We have discussed these symptoms earlier.

MILNE Library mentioned that there's a stage in the process of dying known as transitioning. Professionals use the word "transitioning" to refer to the interval between the actively dying stage and the approaching stage. In this stage, dying people start isolating themselves from their surroundings to prepare for their death. This could entail losing enthusiasm for daily tasks, having less contact with others, and acknowledging the existence of objects and beings that doctors, friends, and relatives cannot see. According to MILNE Library, this is known as "facing death awareness," and health professionals frequently describe it as "hallucinations." The medical profession has proposed hypoxia, acidosis, or changes in metabolic pathways as potential causes of this condition.

The actual death takes two forms, according to health professionals. These include clinical and biological death. The moment a patient's heart ceases to beat is when they experience clinical death. When the heartbeat stops, the flow of blood and breathing also ceases. Cardiopulmonary resuscitation is still adequate at this point to revive victims. It is possible to administer oxygen, maintain blood circulation, and even restore the heartbeat. Most individuals who are near death choose not to opt for the resuscitation option; hence cardiopulmonary resuscitation is hardly administered (MILNE Library). According to studies, resuscitation doesn't work to restart a person's pulse while suffering from a life-threatening illness.

Dying individuals can still be rescued with cardiopulmonary resuscitation for a maximum of Four to Six minutes. Without resuscitation, neurones in the brain would start to deteriorate from oxygen deprivation following clinical death (the end of heartbeat). This is referred to as biological death. It is also known as the end of the road. Once the brain cell dies, cardiopulmonary resuscitation cannot revive the individual. Other cells, including those in the kidneys or the eyes, will also break. Postmortem rigidity happens a few moments after biological death. As defined by Vedantu, postmortem rigidity is the term for the body's muscles and joints becoming tight after someone has passed away. This rigidity typically lasts for one to four days. It is the third phase and a visible sign of mortality that happens due to chemical alterations in the muscles that result in the stiffness of limb muscles.

FROM LOSS TO GRIEF

As a teenager, it's common to feel wounded by losing a loved one when they pass away. Loss is frequently compared to an open, aching sore that needs to mend. The agony of losing a parent is initially very acute, just like the ache from a bodily injury. Any action is a reminder that the damage is still there and consumes all your thoughts. Relatives may have to pay additional attention to look out for you and be present at this initial stage because you can be so absorbed with your injuries. Grief is frequently compared to the process of recovering from an injury. In the right circumstances, the pain will eventually mend on its own.

However, there are occasions when a wound is too severe to admit or treat, so time may not usually mend the way we would. Untreated injuries can grow infected, which makes the anguish of loss more significant. It is essential to treat an infected wound if you want it to recover. Taking care of your grief and promoting its healing involves speaking about what occurred and how you reacted. A significant injury still creates a scar; this does not make the damage disappear. But as years and events pass, it becomes a part of you and stops hurting as much.

THINGS ARE NEVER THE SAME AFTER A LOSS

After somebody we love passes away, vacations are rarely the same. The seemingly unimportant details of an anniversary or holiday gatherings, such as a vacant space at the family dinner or one less present to buy, can act as incredible memories of how drastically our lives have been affected. It can be tough to get used to the idea that we won't ever get to enjoy time with our beloved ones again. Even if the loss was anticipated, you might feel an array of feelings when it happens. There is no natural sequence to the grieving process; however, many people describe experiencing an initial phase of sadness when first hearing of a death.

It is never easy to experience a loved one's demise. The situations of a loss, wildly unexpected or tragic, affect your feelings. Your connection to the deceased individual also affects how you respond. For instance, when a kid dies, an enormous sense of unfairness arises because of unrealised potential, dreams, and unnecessary suffering. Regardless of how unreasonable it may appear, parents feel like they are to blame for their child's passing. Additionally, parents could feel like they have lost a significant aspect of their identity.

The loss of a spouse could likewise be quite devastating. Suppose the deceased was the family's primary means of livelihood. In that case, the demise could result in severe financial problems with a profound psychological impact. The living spouse may need to make substantial interpersonal adjustments following the loss, including learning to parent independently, adjusting to a lone lifestyle, and possibly going back to work. Due to the loss of an entire life of collective memories, older folks may be particularly susceptible when their spouse passes away. Losing intimate friends in this period may make you feel even more alone. One of the most challenging deaths to cope with is a death brought on by suicide. The survivors might be left with a heavy weight of regret, resentment and disgrace. The survivors could even feel guilty for the demise. However, therapy is beneficial and advised during the initial weeks following the suicide.

THE CHALLENGES OF LOSING ONE'S MOTHER AS A TEENAGER

Most individuals will have the most challenging life experience: losing a mother. This incident will probably significantly affect one's life, regardless of whether you had an excellent connection, a problematic relationship, or both. You are probably lamenting the bond you shared, the one you wish you shared with the mother who gave birth to you or even that of a guardian who helped raise you. Since we were not nurtured in societies with many caregivers, mothers have played a significant role in our lives in recent times. According to contemporary psychologists, children naturally need to become attached to anyone who shows them love and cares for them.

In most cases, mothers fit well into this role. Contemporary psychologists believe that a bond is created solely on caring and receptivity, in contrast to the earlier psychologists. The latter thought the bond was driven by food. So it appeals to reason that grieving such a bond or loss would be pretty challenging.

The effect of trauma on children and adolescents relies much on the life stage in which the incident happens. Although people continue to evolve and grow throughout their lives, no other growth stage is more likely to impact a person's behaviour than childhood and teenage years. This viewpoint suggests that each child's developmental stage will have a different impact on the consequences and interpretations of a significant loss. A study by the Institute of Medicine (US) Committee for the Study of Health Consequences of the Stress of Bereavement in 1984 put forward that the frequency with which severe adolescent grief tends to lead to psychosis has generally astounded psychiatrists and many others.

Due to their limited capacity to handle intense emotions for long periods, young kids often alternate between confronting and avoiding their feelings to prevent becoming overwhelmed. Losses can become so distressing and terrifying to them. These feelings could not be recognised as related to grief since they might manifest as irrational conduct or furious tantrums instead of as grief. Moreover, young kids generally transition from grieving reactions to a rapid quest for and acceptance of substitute people because their wants to be catered for and attached to are significant and urgent.

Youngsters are likely to exhibit behaviours and attitudes related to grief for several years after a loss, unlike grown-ups who can only handle a few months or a year of severe distress. This is because they typically revisit, evaluate, and deal with their various strong responses to the loss as they age. As a result, it's crucial to understand the unique characteristics of children's grief and not assume that they will display their feelings in the same ways that grown-ups do or that their outward behaviours will automatically indicate how they feel within. This is from personal experience, anyway.

The loss of a parent can significantly impact a teenager's life. More so with the loss of a mother. The early experiences of a teen are heavily reliant on maternal care and supervision. It could be very challenging for a teen to deal with grief when losing a mom. Different difficulties can arise when teens are grieving. Adolescents may not agree on what it signifies for them to have buried a mother, and neither may others who are attempting to assist them fully comprehend their sadness. Because of the particular difficulties that teenagers face as they leap into adulthood, it can be challenging for adults to provide grief and loss counselling to teenagers. When a teenager loses a mother, you should consider various vital things.

Teenage children who lose their mothers can experience feelings of insecurity and uneasiness. These difficulties surface when a tragedy shakes the structure of their family to its base. They could have feelings of disorientation and loneliness and struggle to put their reliance on people around them. The first approach in helping kids deal with the aftermath of their loss is to understand how sorrow hurts them. They might go through various things, such as extreme alterations in attitudes. It is usually unclear whether a teen struggles to deal with their loss. Although each adolescent may have a different definition of attitudinal alteration or change, you can generally tell when a kid acts differently from how they typically do.

Grief denial is the extraordinary lengths teenagers will go to avoid facing their suffering. They could also experience extremely high pressure. Youngsters may feel overburdened as they try to balance their sadness with their commitments to academics or other responsibilities. They'll often add this extra burden on themselves to avoid facing their grief. They'll develop unhealthy levels of rivalry with their peers, in the classroom or games, and even with the stepmom at home (in case the father remarries). They might have over-whelming feelings, predominantly presented in inappro-priate ways and require parental assistance or counselling to manage.

An adolescent who has lost a mother is likely to experience various emotions, including depression and detachment. When a teen is grieving, they usually isolate themselves from their peers and relatives. To absorb the death of their mother, teenagers may occasionally have to withdraw from friends and hobbies. When a teenager's mother dies, they may have grieving depression, which will eventually pass. Clinical Depression does not get better over time.

Guilt is another emotion commonly felt by grieving teenagers. After facing a significant loss, it's normal to go through various stages of sorrow. Guilt could be part of this stage, and it can take many different shapes. Let's take, for example, the survivor's guilt. This is a type of guilt that is frequently experienced during grief. In situations where you survive a car crash or another form of accident, just because you took an unconscious step that maybe someone else could have taken, you might subsequently feel bad that your beloved one died rather than you. Adolescents may behave strangely due to the sorrow they are going through. Adolescents may be in a more vulnerable position when suffering appears, and they move through various phases because of their changing emotions brought on by puberty and other physiological and mental changes that are already occurring.

Survival guilt can have the following effects on teenagers.

*W*ishing for death: When individuals express their desire to pass away, they often do not mean it in the strictest sense. These emotions are a normal response to grief and typically pass unnoticed. These are only thoughts if you don't have a course of strategy to put them into action. When your ideas are causing you to have positive intentions to act, you might want to think about online counselling or grief therapy.

· · ·

*D*rug addiction: Some mourning teenagers overuse alcohol and drugs to block away the unpleasant feelings they are experiencing. Some teenagers find it impossible to cope with grief after losing a mother since the anguish can be overpowering.

*D*ropping grades or skipping class: Grief can make you believe nothing in your life is essential, including attending class and completing schoolwork. Most of the time, this lack of concentration on school is brief and reasonable when a parent has passed away.

*P*romiscuous behaviour: When the sadness leaves you feeling empty, it's not unusual to seek comfort in another individual's embrace. Even while these emotions are merely transient, they have the potential to trigger more extensive problems. Occasionally loneliness might cloud your judgment. Think of more strategies to fill this gap. Consider adopting a pet after you are ready to care for one. A pet offers unwavering affection, company, and psychological support.

WHAT A GRIEVING TEENAGER MIGHT NEED

Adequate Information: Provide your kid with sufficient knowledge by giving them the specifics of their mother's demise in digestible pieces and in a precise, straightforward manner. Be clear about what they can experience in the days or weeks after losing a mom. The most vital point is to neither conceal nor postpone reality. Although it is customary to desire to shield your kid, it is better to be open and straightforward. In addition to building their confidence in you, informing your kid what occurred will aid in their ability to deal with their loss. Look for a secure and peaceful area where you can talk to your kids and prepare your remarks. Invite the kids to sit beside you. Allow the minor child to keep their favourite item, doll, or comforter if available. Give them enough time to comprehend by speaking gently and pausing frequently. This approach will also offer you the opportunity to control your own emotions.

Addressing youngsters of all ages, be understanding and truthful, but when speaking to small kids, be extra straightforward and avoid using code words. A small kid will be more perplexed if you utter stuff like, "We lost a rare gem," because they won't comprehend what that implies. Parents might benefit more by saying, "I have some terrible news to give." Then, with warmth and tenderness, continue, "Mom has passed away. That indicates that her organs and body ceased functioning, and we won't see her anymore." Although it can be challenging for fathers to speak straightforwardly, it's crucial to be open and truthful.

You must give them a little moment to process this news. Young kids may respond by acting like they're not listening. Wait for their utmost attention while being calm. Additionally, be ready for smaller kids to keep asking similar questions right at the moment and in a few days to come. Keep an eye out for any "mystical" thoughts. Some kids could be concerned that some words they uttered contributed to the tragedy. Check to discover whether they have any concerns because kids of all levels may seem guilty. You could subtly ask: "Are you concerned that something you spoke or did, caused mom to pass away?" Inform them of what occurred in straightforward language and comfort them that nothing about what happened is their fault. For instance, you could say: "You didn't do anything wrong. Mommy became ill from a bacterium, which also caused her to become unresponsive and dead. It was possible for her to catch it anywhere, which was no one's fault, and none of us could do anything about that."

Teenagers may need assistance in coping with their loss. Still, they typically find it easier to talk to others who have experienced similar things. Introducing your kid to their classmates is beneficial so that they can exchange perspectives. Think about looking for neighbourhood support networks through your local chapel, college, or other grief support networks online or in your neighbourhood. Discuss with your child and let them know that experiencing loss is common for people. Over time, they'll develop coping mechanisms and finally begin to feel well. Discuss the fundamental ideas of dying and what it signifies to them. It is important to reaffirm to them the four notions of death. First, although it might seem apparent to you, death is inevitable. In light of this, you should also discuss how all biological activities cease entirely at death. Third, it is a simple fact that all living things will someday pass away. Finally, there could be physical or medical causes of death.

Teenagers who suffer a significant loss could express their grief more distinctively than grown-ups. For young kids, the loss of a mother can be especially traumatic and impact their sense of safety or ability to survive. They frequently question the transformations they observe everywhere around them, especially if concerned adults attempt to shield them from the facts or the sadness of the other parent still alive. Kids relatively young have distinct difficulty due to their limited comprehension and inability to articulate their emotions. Small kids could regress to prior habits (like bedwetting), pose inappropriate inquiries about the dead, create scenarios about dying, or act as though the loss never occurred.

A grieving parent feels additional stress as they deal with their kid's grief. But yelling or criticism makes a child feel more anxious and slows their healing. Instead, communicate openly with them in a language they can comprehend. Spend more time discussing loss and the deceased with them. Help children process their emotions and remember that they rely on adults for appropriate conduct.

You watch your reactions and emotions as a surviving parent: Your reaction as a surviving parent largely influences how your kids will deal with their grief about the loss. Kids turn to their parents to be their source of unwavering love and protection from the unpleasant truths of living. When a mother passes away, the child's life frequently gets incredibly frightening and unclear, causing the child to worry about what will happen next. Naturally, this puts a lot of pressure on the father, who is still alive, and other relatives who wish to support the child as they cope with the loss of the departed soul. Some cultures have a favourable outlook on grief; some, on the other hand, advise adults to suppress their feelings in the presence of youngsters who are grieving. These cultures frequently argue that youngsters turn to their elders to be resilient during uncertain times to defend their emotions.

While writing *Parenting for Brain,* Pamela Li classified these emotions into repressing and suppressing. Repressed emotions are the body's effort to get rid of opposing ideas. Making an intentional and purposeful effort to hide feelings from other people is known as suppressing emotions. When a parent or caregiver is upset, they may prefer to keep it to themselves to avoid upsetting their kid. Repressed feelings frequently go unobserved; it emanates spontaneously. People who are repressed might not be aware of their feelings at the moment of occurrence. These suppressed feelings could release themselves in the future. However, studies have shown that it impedes the recovery process for both the caregiver and the child. A particular study, however, reveals that suppressed feelings have a protective function during the grieving period.

It's still debatable if a parent repressing or suppressing their emotions is a healthy healing strategy. Suppression or repression by a parent might or might not benefit the parent's psychological health. However, what matters most is how their attitudes toward emotional denial influence how they support their kid in coping with the grief. The issue of death is often avoided in the household. Parents who have survived the tragedy often act "natural" around the child because they believe youngsters are incapable of comprehending death or adequately coping with the feelings it entails. But the reality is that the steps taken by the surviving parent in those periods that come immediately after the bereavement can help children cope with the loss in a healthy way.

Surviving parents or caregivers of grieving kids can use the following methods to assist them in dealing effectively instead of acting as though everything was excellent.

*M*ake the grieving journey look normal: The impact of a mother's loss on a kid relies on how well the significant adults in their life respond to the loss. It's critical to normalise the grieving journey. A youngster who has lost a mother should be taught that expressing feelings and talking about the deceased is okay. It enables children to lessen future anxiety. After a mother passes away, children may experience various emotions, including wrath and remorse. They must understand that children are never to blame for the death. Also common is the child's perception that their departed mother is present in their dreams or visions. They are not required to disregard their dead mother.

*I*mplement good parenting: Children frequently misbehave to express their challenges in coping with the transformations brought on by the loss. Fathers can foster a good father-child bond and an atmosphere that promotes clear communication by practising good parenting. Warmth and encouragement are characteristics of good parenting dads. Appropriate constructive punishment is used, and the father is compassionate and strict. After a mother dies, children's transition can be aided by efficient, good parenting. It lowers the risk of paediatric mental illnesses, including major psychiatric disorders, and encourages grieving children to adapt quickly.

*L*imit children's access to harmful situations: Following the death of a mother, unpleasant life occurrences are associated with a rise in children's mental health issues—for instance, the initial two years after a loss and summer vacations. Parents who listen well can give their kids a secure setting to express their views about the holiday. Grieving children frequent can be challenging for grieving households, particularly for the kids who worry when their fathers start dating and form new, long-term romantic relationships. Fathers might gradually present a new female relative or spouse. They should be honest and age-appropriate while discussing the connection with their kids.

*D*evelop child coping abilities: After one or both parents pass away, employing practical coping skills is linked to more favourable adaption. These tactics may involve optimism and rephrasing unfavourable self-made assertions into more favourable ones. You could help in assisting them in recognising occurrences they can manage and assisting them in letting go of the idea that they can work unmanageable affairs. Additionally, you ought to assist them in concentrating on problem-solving and searching out mental assistance to cope with challenging circumstances.

Surviving parents might ask their kids to create objectives for exercising these abilities to help grieving kids feel more empowered. When the children employ these methods, they can offer precise good feedback. Additionally, parents should continually affirm their faith in their kids' capacity for prob-lem-solving. Compared to their classmates who have not experienced a loss, grieving youngsters may feel more powerless and think they have less influence over what happens to them. Focusing on educating kids about their duties can help them handle this worry after losing a mother at an early age. By emphasising the differences between issues that are the kid's duty to solve and issues that are the duty of adults, you can help children develop an adaptive feeling of responsibility.

For instance, if the surviving parent is having difficulty dealing with the grief personally, they may first be open and straightforward with the children about their troubles. The parent can now inform the children that they will consult a qualified specialist rather than expecting the children to assist them. Learning that the parent's priority is better to handle their grief and the children's focus is to concentrate on their school work and hanging out with friends will benefit the children.

*E*nsure adequate support is provided mainly for individuals outside the family. Many individuals think that teenagers have loving families and loved ones who will always be there for them. This might not be accurate in practice. The teenager's societal demands and the absence of available help are frequently related. Typically, they are assumed to be "grown-ups" and help the other relatives, especially the surviving parent and the younger siblings. Many teenagers have heard the statement, "Now you must look after your family." Teenagers who feel like they need to "look after the family" are deprived of the chance and freedom to grieve.

We frequently presume that youngsters will seek solace among their peers. However, this could not hold if it pertains to loss. Many grieving teenagers encounter a lack of interest in their friends. Friends tend to convey their emotions of powerlessness by avoiding all talk of loss, except when they have personally faced it. Please remember that many grieving teenagers live in settings that do not offer help and support while we work to help them. They can ask for help, only to hear "life goes on, just get going with it" from mates and relatives.

You might consider linking the teenager with a support network in situations like this. One of the best ways to aid grieving teenagers in their recovery is through support networks. Teenagers who are part of a group can interact with other teenagers who have also suffered a loss. They are free to share their experiences as frequently and in as many ways as possible. Several people in this situation will be eager to admit that loss has permanently altered their lives. Teenagers may need your assistance in locating such a network.

The support network is essential because challenges in relationships could exist after a teenager suffers a considerable loss, such as the loss of a mother. Teenagers typically distance themselves from their families during a moment of devaluation, albeit it can be a complex process. Their attempt to become independent frequently leads to clashes with their families. There is often a feeling of shame and "unresolved issues" if a mother passes away. At the same time, the teenager physically and mentally drives the deceased mother off their mind. We can see how this affects the feeling of grieving, even though the desire to remove oneself from the loss is common. We know that most teenagers go through challenging periods with their parents and family. Disputes arise naturally as an outcome of the act of developing an identity separate from their parents. A natural urge to discuss their connection with the deceased might arise after death when mixed with child-parent and family connections stress.

𝒲rapping Up

The teenage loss of a mother will profoundly impact your life and permanently transform you. Everybody will experience a loved one's loss at some point in their lifetimes, but losing a mother while still in their teenage years can be tremendously traumatic. Numerous things will probably shift in your life. Still, eventually, a new routine for you will develop, and your grief will start to fade.

Investigate the range of supportive options available in your neighbourhood to assist a teenager struggling severely with their grief. Some teenagers may benefit from school psychologists, church organisations, and private counsellors. In contrast, others may only require a little extra love and concern from kind grown-ups like you. The most vital point is that you support the bereaved kid in finding supportive emotional avenues during this trying time.

Remember that losing a loved one can be a devastating experience for a teenager. The teen's life is being rebuilt as a direct consequence of the loss. Keep the gravity of the loss when assisting and exercise kindness and compassion. Grief is complicated. Depending on the teen, it will differ. Teenagers need to hear from caring grown-ups that this emotion is normal and nothing to be embarrassed about or conceal. Instead, grieving is normal for humans to show their affection for a deceased loved one. Responsible grown-ups face a distinct dilemma because kids do not have an option between mourning and not mourning. In contrast, adults have a choice regarding whether or not to assist teenagers in coping with their loss.

GRIEF AND ITS FIVE STAGES

*M*any incorrectly think that grief is only one feeling. Still, it is a robust, complex and frequently overwhelming reaction that people go through after a terrible or unpleasant event like losing a parent. We can experience grief's physical, psychological, and even spiritual effects. You might feel the impact of grief both psychologically and physically. You might undergo several physiological signs during this period that are typical of the grieving process.

It can be nice to be a human. We are social beings who long for close relationships with our loved ones. The most fulfilling aspects of existence can be found in such relationships. Strong partnerships, however, come with the risk of suffering a setback. One of the most challenging experiences a person can have is grief. Individuals who have experienced the great anguish and despair brought on by the loss of a parent are familiar with this sensation. The brain, which generates our feelings, is the appropriate place to look for an explanation for why we experience grief the way we do.

GRIEF AND THE HUMAN BRAIN

You could go through many psychological and emotional shifts following losing a loved one. You might occasionally discover that you're just confused, unable to concentrate, or walking in circles. It may appear stressful, unattainable, or take longer to do everyday or easy activities. Your effective time management between workplace and home before your loved one passed away has mysteriously vanished, together with your positive coping mechanisms and capacity to handle stress. You might have been a master in checking and balances, but you are now incapable of adding one-to-one. You either find out you've cleared a bill repeatedly or forget the deadline.

The brain is adept at finding solutions to issues. In actuality, the brain serves this purpose. In her book *The Grieving Brain: The Surprising Science of How We Learn from Love and Loss*, Mary-Frances O'Connor explains that she concluded after decades of study that the brain spends much time tracing the whereabouts of our loved ones. At the same time, they're still living, so we can locate them in an emergency. Additionally, the brain frequently prioritises familiar knowledge over new knowledge. However, it is challenging to comprehend new fundamental knowledge, such as losing our dear parents. When grieving, we must face the challenging work of changing our connection with the deceased and discarding the road map we used to steer our lives jointly. Without making this change, many things would be disrupted in line with our daily existence. Things that seem relatively easy might suddenly become difficult.

Although you had several things you "intended to accomplish," it now appears you may go weeks without accomplishing anything. When travelling to known locations, you frequently get confused on arrival and question, "how did I arrive here?" You might overlook upcoming engagements, planned activities, or well-known names. You might lose your personal belongings more frequently, only to find them later in unexpected places (such as the car key in the kitchen cabinet or your wallet in the fridge). When attempting to make everyday decisions, your perception could appear confused.

It will likely take some time before your grief-related memory lapses stop and your mental ability returns to its original state. Although it might not be something you wanted to hear, keep in mind that your brain has gone through trauma on a physiological level. Making sense of things that will never make sense is something that all those cognitive pathways that used to function so strongly are desperately attempting to do. It takes minimal brain energy when your thoughts push so hard to keep a record of more than one book passage. Or to recollect that your Television remote control belongs to the living room and not in the refrigerator. When you're grieving after a loss, it's difficult to think clearly and concisely.

These are typical signs of the effect of grief on your brain. Do not be alarmed; this is a regular aspect of grieving. Your mind is overflowing with ideas of sorrow, solitude, and other negative emotions. The grieving reason impacts your memories, focus, and cognitive abilities. Your attention is mainly on the signs and emotions of mourning, which offers little brain capacity for routine tasks. Being kind and compassionate with oneself is crucial. Expecting to carry out your basic activities as you did before your loved one passed away may be unrealistic or unattainable. Be careful to create realistic assumptions, then go from there. Try giving yourself a high-five after you finish a chore and acknowledge it as a stride on the road to recovery.

Note down important information on a pad of paper or tablet so you can easily refer to it later. This will help you concentrate. Sticky notes may not be helpful because they can get unstuck and disappear. When assistance is required, inquire. Take many naps. Say encouraging things out loud.

The myriad of emotions you have can be revealed through journaling, which is an excellent treatment. Well, these are just a few things to whet your appetite. We will be discussing more in the subsequent chapters. However, there are a few things to note about the relationship of grief with the brain. Let's discuss them.

One way of learning is through grief: According to O'Connor, if a loved one passes away, your brain attempts to find a solution. Your brain is constantly trying to forecast what will occur next. And so, as you hugged your parents farewell every day as they left for the office, you became accustomed to anticipating that they would be absent for a few moments before returning. It doesn't make a reasonable assumption to think they're completely gone when you've been together for a long time. And you open up one Monday morning, and your parent isn't there to bid you the usual goodbye. The brain must comprehend the information your parent won't be returning before determining what this means for your life. That implies that either your father will no longer have a wife or you won't go on vacation together. Learning how that will operate takes much time.

.   .   .

*D*epression and grief are distinct emotions: According to O'Connor, grief is primarily char-acterised by a strong desire for your loved one to return and for circumstances to return to how they were. Grief is mainly a longing emotion with a particular individual serving as the object. She said that depression is universal and not simply about the deceased person. You believe that there are addi-tional ways in which the universe is not fair, that you are not doing enough, or that others dislike you. The depression wouldn't go away even if the departed individual came back.

The loss of someone we love, the termination of employ-ment, or the dissolution of a union are all trying events for a person to go through. It is common for people to experience sadness or grief in reaction to such circumstances. People who have lost something frequently label themselves as "depressed." But in reality, being depressed does not share relations with grief. The grieving journey is average, partic-ular to each person, and shares some characteristics with depression. However, extreme sadness and detachment are familiar in both grieving and depression.

Making the distinction between grief and depression is crucial because it can help victims get the assistance or care they require. Grieving people keep their emotions to them-selves and avoid talking about them, which can harm recov-ery. You'll get better if you discuss your issues and permit yourself to experience sadness. After a loss, counselling allows you to examine your feelings and discover constructive coping mechanisms.

*Y*our **brain must gain valuable experience and patience before it can comprehend the loss:** O'Connor claims in her publication that after the passing away of the person you love, your brain must refresh its internal global map. It doesn't happen suddenly; instead, it develops over time as you continually go through the daily activities you undertake alone. She claims that you will discover that the deceased person didn't attend meals on thirty-one occasions after a month. Grief lasts considerably longer than thirty-one days, so nothing is magical about that. Still, throughout that month, your brain will begin to get updates. O'Connor, during her grieving period, attached a note on her kitchen wall reminding her to cook, do some cleaning, engage in activities, and she should play. It was a helpful reminder for her to focus on life's essentials and set realistic goals for herself.

Grief requires patience, commitment, and tolerance. This idea is crucial in dealing with loss and sadness since it can lead to significant growth to redirect your mental energy into something constructive and helpful. People become unclear about how to use their energies as the emotions of mourning start to lessen. However, developing poor habits now could exacerbate the issue and prolong the grieving process.

*S*upport is crucial when suffering from brain grief: Having a support network is one factor that can significantly impact how your brain handles grief. Support has two significant advantages: it affords you more space for grieving and greater confidence in your capacity for adaptation. Being without your loved one requires you to adjust to a different way of life, which makes grieving a lengthy process. Grief management is an ongoing process that takes years. Grief can strike whenever a memory does, often in a fresh way. Grief gradually gets easier to handle, even though it can initially feel insurmountable.

GRIEF AND THE HUMAN BODY

It may seem like there is little you can do to speed up the process. When we discuss grief, psychological and mental well-being frequently play a crucial role. But grief can also have significant bodily impacts. Knowing the physical shifts that occur while you grieve can help you maintain control over your health, even if recovery requires a lot of time.

Even while our bodily health may not be in distress after losing a loved one, there is no doubt that our mental health may seem in pain. The central nervous system goes into a frenzy due to our body's reaction to stress. Our body is attempting to shield us rather than harm us. Our body is merely bracing for the fight or flight reaction when faced with a challenge, which is what decades of development and survival have shown to be optimal for us.

THE REACTION OF FIGHT OR FLIGHT

Honestly, the physical body is incredible. The body's components work together to provide a quick and continual reaction to changes in the surroundings and inside the body. The body reacts to threats by producing hormones that will aid in responding to the threat. The objective is to provide oxygenated blood to the areas of the body that require it most. In a situation where all that is needed is to run, your heart and the powerful leg muscles want oxygen. It would help if you had it so that your brain and perceptive systems could process as many facts as required before responding to the threat.

The body's release of catecholamines is one of its reactions to bodily or psychological pressure. *Medical News Today* noted that the adrenal glands, brain, and nervous system all create catecholamines as hormones when under stress, either physically or emotionally. The three major categories of these hormones are dopamine, adrenaline, and noradrenaline. While adrenaline is in charge of the fight-or-flight reaction, dopamine is responsible for regulating emotion, moods, cognition, and the brain's reward system. Stress causes the body to create adrenaline, which increases blood circulation to the heart, lungs, and muscles. Finally, noradrenaline aids in the body's reaction to anxiety. A person's pulse rate rises as a result of noradrenaline secretion.

Additionally, it affects mood management and concentration. These hormones' secretions increase the heartbeat and pulse rate, blood is diverted to the muscles, respiration becomes faster, and digestion slows down. The force you require is delivered where it is most needed. Even the pupils enlarge to allow you to see more of the potential hazard.

The release of corticosteroids, or stress hormones, is a different reaction to sensed threats. These hormones improve your body's natural ability to obtain stored energy, prevent the production of antibodies, and control sodium retention. Instead of waging a protracted battle against sickness, the body is getting vitality accessible for use and concentrating on the immediate threat. In other words, the immune system is weakened, and regular processes are interfered with due to the body's reaction to an impending risk. These reactions are understandable from a survival standpoint, but they might not be helpful in the long run, particularly if we have recently lost a loved one. This reaction may not be healthy and may even have negative consequences on the body.

How physically challenging grieving can be is fantastic. Your heart hurts so bad. You recall something that makes your tummy turn or sends a shiver through your spine. Sometimes you can hardly fall asleep because your body is so charged with energy that it causes your mind and pulse to speed. Sometimes you're so exhausted that you nod off right away. The following morning, you awaken, still highly worn out, and spend most of the day lying down helpless. Let's expand more on the effects of grief on the body.

Gastrointestinal issues and body-weight changes: Grief can result in momentary digestive problems such as bloating, diarrhoea, stomach cramps, a "feeling of emptiness" in the belly, stomach ache, or feeling nauseated, which are frequently linked to the alteration of usual dietary behaviours or patterns. A lot of people experience weight changes. Many individuals tend to gain weight in the weeks, months, and years after a loss. Binge eating, eating out more frequently, consuming more sugary snacks, not exercising enough, and not taking care of oneself can all contribute to weight changes. Separation from family members who could otherwise support better or more dependable eating patterns could also be an issue.

Abnormalities in digestion can be attributed to blood being diverted from the gastrointestinal tract in favour of the mind, brain, sensory receptors, and big muscles in the legs, which are the body's primary survival systems. It's also noteworthy that many individuals "undereat," skip food, or choose not to taste anything while grieving. Grieving families may find the variety of actions and arrangements that must be made—as well as the arrival of family and friends in the first few days or weeks after the loss and end up forgetting to eat regularly.

*P*ain, uneasiness, or discomfort: Serious pain or discomfort, such as difficulty breathing, moderate to solid headaches, stiffness in the arms and legs, pains in the shoulder, spine, or bone joints, or general muscle aches, can be brought on by the emotion of grieving a loss. Grief and the sorrow of losing a loved one can weaken or suppress the immune response, leaving you more vulnerable to diseases and pathogens. According to one research published in the *Circulation Journal* in 2012, persons with a high heart disease risk may be more prone to cardiac arrest in the moments following the loss of a loved one.

· · ·

*H*eart problems, various ailments, and a higher mortality rate are all predicted by inflammation: Additionally, those who already have a chronic illness may worsen their conditions. Increased inflammatory reaction in the body has also been related to grieving.

The flight or fight reflex has the potential to impact circulation as well. When blood is diverted to the bigger muscles, there may be less blood flow to the appendages (the fingertips and toes). As a result, you get a sensation of extreme cold in your toes and palms. Debilitating headaches are another side effect of the circulatory systems responding to distress. When you eventually get some downtime, you may suffer these migraines, which vision difficulties can identify, hypersensitivity to light and noise, and even vomiting! According to this theory, if our blood vessels widen excessively due to our body's prolonged response to distress in our circulatory system, the body would recover when we eventually rest. The pounding ache is the effect of pressure being placed on the nearby tissue.

The circulatory system doesn't often respond to the trauma of losing a loved one the most severely. Some individuals' reactions include weak respiration. In other terms, they breathe more than usual. When we live on oxygen in low amounts, we can experience floating, twitching in our lips, fingertips, and soles of the feet, and even dizziness. This may not even be noticeable to others. Many individuals become nervous and breathe more quickly and thinly when they see evidence of breathlessness, which worsens the symptoms. If we frequently find ourselves sighing, that may be a sign that we are engaging in this behaviour. This is an attempt by our body to counteract the adverse effects of breathlessness.

*S*leep issues: A mourning person may not get the therapeutic advantages of a whole night's rest due to insomnia. This sleep deprivation can have an aesthetic impact by making the eyes and face look puffy. Inadequate sleep brought on by grief frequently affects pulse rate, brain function, and bodily coordination. While getting enough sleep is a necessary part of everyday life, napping for long periods or all day can deplete your vitality and make you feel lazy.

The body and mind are designed to rest and repair during sleep. Sleeping provides a haven that frequently enables grievers to flee the anguish of loss momentarily. It might be highly frustrating when grieving prevents you from sleeping. Being perpetually upset, worried, and worn out can be crippling. People who are grieving have insomnia. Whether a person in grief typically sleeps too much or decides to take extended naps, they might not feel fully rested after several hours of rest. While grieving can make you feel worn out, this does not necessarily guarantee that falling asleep will be simple. Mourning people frequently have trouble falling asleep. They are more prone to suffer from middle insomnia, which is difficulty falling asleep after waking at midnight. These sleep issues are frequently a direct outcome of the significant shifts accompanying grief, such as overwhelming emotions of solitude or concerns about future financial stability.

*C*hallenges in performing daily tasks: Grief's physical effects can make it challenging to manage daily tasks. For instance, you can suffer signs of exhaustion or anxiety that make it difficult to handle everyday duties. Symptoms of nervousness or anxiety include tapping your fingertips, moving to and fro, restlessness, being unable to sit still for extended periods, wet or cold hands or feet, or sensations of prickling or cramping in those limbs. Mentally, you can experience brain fog, often known as being easily confused or having trouble focusing. This is more of an effect on the brain, but the result is on body productivity. For instance, you might find yourself trying to remember names or some other essential details when narrating a story. You might also discover needing to read the same email repeatedly at work to comprehend the intended message.

WHEN ARE ALL THESE REACTIONS GOING TO IMPROVE?

The duration of loss-related physical symptoms is difficult to anticipate, just as grieving doesn't have a set schedule. These reactions will be at their worst immediately following the passing of your loved one. However, they usually get reduced with time. Nevertheless, some individuals suffer symptoms in cycles; they may feel great for a few months before suffering a relapse as their grief resurfaces in their thoughts. This is quite natural and merely indicates that you still need to grieve.

Be kind to yourself as you recognise your tendencies. While you cannot control or foresee how grieving may manifest, remember that it is a journey guiding you toward more robust tolerance and wellness. As symptoms emerge or return, seek the healthcare attention you require in the intervening time. Don't be afraid to contact an expert if you discover that your grief is too overwhelming for you to manage. Grief therapists can assist you in developing a tailored strategy to deal with the extreme sorrow you are now going through.

Grief has the power to disrupt our lives completely. So it is crucial to be conscious of all the aspects it may be impacting you psychologically, emotionally and physiologically. You should also give yourself the most tender, loving care your body requires. Self-care practices like going for walks in nature, going to bed consistently, feeding well, and drinking plenty of water can be very effective while grieving. Try to include these in your routine as often as possible to improve your wellness. Continue to be patient and fair to yourself as you've always been.

WHAT TASKS DOES GRIEF PERFORM?

The abbreviation "TEAR" is used by William Worden to explain the four grieving "tasks," which are described in his model of grief. Worden's responsibilities are not in any particular order, and as you manage to accept your loss, you must repeatedly switch between them as you go through the mourning process.

T: **To acknowledge the actuality of the loss.** Realising that your dear one has passed away is the first step in embracing failure. In the initial stages, it is customary to desire to ignore what has occurred, possibly to save yourself the suffering of the loss. When a loved one passes away tragically, either in a disaster or by euthanasia, it can often be tough to comprehend the loss. Because it can prevent you from recognising the truth of their passing, you might not like to consider how they passed away. Avoidance, however, prevents grief and, over time, may worsen your feelings. Whenever anyone passes away, routines and cere-monies can assist you in coming to terms with the fact that they are no longer physically present.

E: **Experience the anguish of loss firsthand.** To do this mission, you must deal with your grief's discomfort. Many people in our society have learned to repress or avoid uncomfortable emotions. Finding a private space to process your feelings might be challenging because everyone around you wants you to be okay. But suppressing our feelings makes them worse and may even prolong our misery. Regarding the emotions you need to handle, there is no set pattern. Everyone experiences grief in a different manner. Worden, like many other experts, also admits that every person experiences loss in a unique way. It's crucial to discover strategies for handling your suffering, no matter its effects on you. This can entail getting therapy or discussing it with reliable individuals.

a: **Adjust to a newfound way of living without the deceased individual.** It may take some time to get used to living without your beloved one, and you could even feel bad about it. Everyone will experience this practice differently. Additionally, it will rely on your connection and how much time you spend next to each other. For instance, losing a close friend who was a great source of help and confidence in your life may need you to develop new relationships and discover new methods to engage in activities you may have previously done together. People who have lost their soul mate can learn ways to do everything they used to do. You could need to acquire new abilities and carry out previously untried tasks.

R: **Reinvest in a fresh start.** As a result of this "reinvestment," the message Worden is trying to pass across is the art of maintaining a strong emotional bond with the departed soul. It doesn't stop there. It summarily entails adjusting to your fresh start while cherishing and letting your departed love continue to exist in your mind and memory. Each individual will interpret this differently. For many individuals, this entails making new friends and doing things that will give their lives a new purpose and enjoyment.

STAGES OF GRIEF

Numerous psychological health professionals and scholars have devoted years to researching loss and the emotions accompanying it to grasp the mourning process better. Elisabeth Kübler-Ross, a Swiss-American psychiatrist, was one of these specialists. She developed the 5 phases of grief and loss model known as the Kübler-Ross model. Kübler-Ross investigated the five most typical mental responses to loss in her 1969 book *"On Death and Dying"*: "denial," "anger," "bargaining," "depression," and "acceptance." were first known as the "five stages of death," according to Kübler-Ross. This was because she was treating terminally ill people during the period, which were the familiar feelings they experienced while contemplating death.

Years after publishing her initial book, Kübler-Ross expanded and modified her approach by considering different types of loss. The five phases of grieving evolved from the five phases of dying. There are many various ways and causes for this grief. Everybody eventually suffers loss and grief, regardless of their background or culture. Dealing with your mortality or the mortality of a loved one is not the only reason to experience distress. Aside from death, other causes of suffering include sickness, the loss of a close friendship, the failure of a mission, or the end of ambition. Now, let's discuss these stages.

1. **Denial:** The first of the five phases of grieving is denial. It enables us to endure the tragedy of loss. The world seems worthless and overpowering at this point. Life is illogical. We're in shock and disbelief during this stage. We feel numb. We ponder whether we can continue, how, and why we ought to. Every day, we strive to find a way to get by. Denial and trauma enable us to adapt and give room for survival. We can limit our grief by denying our sensations of loss. Rejection has elegance to it. Nature uses this only to take in what we can manage.

You unconsciously commence the healing process when you begin to acknowledge the truth of the circumstances you're facing at the moment and pose yourself with different questions. A typical defence strategy is denial. The denial is fading, and you are gaining strength. However, as you continue, all the emotions you had been suppressing come to the forefront. Your instant shock at the unpleasant circumstance might be lessened with its aid. You can initially have second thoughts about the actuality of the loss as an initial response. Here are a few instances of this kind of denial:

- When a loved one passes away, you could find yourself daydreaming that someone would phone to say there was an error and nothing occurred.
- When going through a breakup, you could tell yourself that your ex-partner would soon change their mind and return to you.
- If you were sacked at work, you could believe that after realising their error, your previous employer would reinstate you.

You can experience a period when nothing seems to appeal to you. The way you used to live has changed. It may be challenging to feel like you can go on. The initial phase of mourning is a normal response that aids in your processing of the loss. After this initial shock and denial-based response, you might feel numb for a moment. By becoming numb, you can give yourself space to investigate the alterations you're passing through at your speed. Denial is a transient reaction that helps you get past the initial surge of agony. The suppressed opinions and feelings will eventually come back to the forefront when you're prepared, and your healing process will resume.

2. **Anger:** A vital stage in the journey of recovery is anger. Although it could seem to last forever, be open to feeling your anger. It will start to go away, and you will begin to heal faster the further you feel it. Although there are numerous other feelings beneath anger, anger is the one we are often accustomed to controlling. The fact is, anger knows no bounds. It can include God in addition to your best friend, the medical staff, your relatives, yourself, and the deceased loved one. Why did God allow this? You might wonder.

Anger hides pain—your pain—under it. Feeling forsaken and neglected is normal, but our society suppresses anger. Anger can be an anchor, providing momentary shape to the void of loss because anger is a powerful emotion. Grief initially resembles being cut off from everything, like feeling lost at sea. Then you become enraged with someone, possibly somebody who didn't participate in the funeral, somebody who has passed away, or somebody who has changed since your loved one passed away. Your resentment toward them has suddenly taken on a structure. The anger serves as a link between you and them, a bridge across the vast ocean.

You might become angrier as a result. You could also experience remorse for just being furious at times. Try to keep in mind that your anger is a symptom of pain. Even though it may not seem like it, this rage is essential for recovery. After distancing yourself from it throughout the denial phase, anger could also be a means to reestablish contact with the outside world. You become estranged from everybody while you're numb. Even if only through this feeling, you relate when you are upset. However, you could feel other emotions throughout this phase besides anger. Possible reactions to your loss include hostility, resentment, worry, frustration, and restlessness. Everything is a component of the very same process.

. . .

3. **Bargaining:** Before a tragedy, it feels as though you would sacrifice anything to save a loved one. You beg God, "Lord, Please, if you'll only let my father live, I'll forever listen to him and not quarrel with him." Following a defeat, negotiation may take the shape of a brief respite. "What if I spend the remainder of my life serving others? If so, may I wake up and understand that everything has been a nightmare? We get disoriented when we start making "Maybe if" or "What if" assertions. We desire the resurrection of our loved ones and a return to the previous state of existence.

If only we could go back in time and detect cancer earlier, diagnose the disease earlier, and prevent the tragedy. Bargaining frequently has guilt as an accomplice. "If only" will lead us to blame ourselves and worry about what we "might have" handled better. We might even barter with the suffering. To avoid the anguish of this death, we shall stop at nothing. We continue to live in the past while attempting to come to terms with the pain. Frequently, people assume that the stages endure a few weeks or even months.

They fail to realise that the stages are reactions to emotions that can linger for several minutes or even hours as we alternate between them. We don't move linearly through each step before leaving it. We might experience one, then the next, and finally, the first one once more. These feelings and

99

ideas are all prevalent. Even though it may be difficult, this aids in your recovery as you face the truth of your loss.

4. **Depression:** After bargaining, our focus is firmly on the moment. Grief permeates our life on a larger scale than we ever thought when empty emotions start to appear. It seems as though this depressed phase will never end. It's critical to realise that such depression does not indicate a psychiatric condition. It is the proper reaction to a significant loss. We get depressed and retreat from life, possibly questioning whether it is worthwhile to continue living alone. Why even continue? You could query. Too frequently, depression following a loss is viewed as an unnatural condition that needs to be repaired or overcome. Your initial thought should be whether or not your circumstance is genuinely depressing. Depression is a common and acceptable reaction to the tragic event of losing a loved one. It would be odd not to feel depressed after a loved one is away. Knowing that such a loved person did not improve this time and would not return is gloomy once a loss has fully settled in your mind. Depression is among the several crucial steps that must be taken in the recovery process of grieving.

Depression is felt in various ways, just like the other phases of grief. There isn't a correct or incorrect way to approach it, and there isn't a timetable to resolve it. You begin to confront your current situation and the inevitable nature of the loss you've endured throughout the depression. This knowledge could make you feel incredibly depressed and hopeless. You can change how you react due to this severe grief. You can feel: worn out, predisposed, perplexed, and preoccupied; unable to move forward; not hungry or eager to eat; hesitant to get up early for work; and unable to take pleasure in the things you used to like. All of this is usually transient and a result of your grief process. Despite how daunting it might feel, this phase is essential in your recovery process.

5. **Acceptance:** Being "all fine" or "okay" with what occurred and acceptance are two concepts that are sometimes misconstrued. The opposite is true. Most individuals never genuinely feel okay or all fine after losing a loved one. At this phase, we must embrace the fact that our loved one is no longer visibly there and acknowledge that this current truth is the only truth that exists. Although we can never enjoy or tolerate this truth, we gradually come to terms with it. We develop coping mechanisms. We must adapt to the new pattern that it represents. We must try to live in the present while our loved one is gone.

Many individuals first desire to keep their lives as they were before a loved one passed away when they oppose this new pattern. But over time, as we gradually accept, we realise that we cannot entirely preserve the previous. We must keep adjusting because it has undergone a permanent change. We must develop the ability to rearrange positions, transfer them to others, or assume them ourselves. Simply spending more great days than unpleasant days could be enough to gain acceptance. We frequently feel we are hurting the deceased individual as we start living again and enjoying our lives. There is nothing we can ever do to make up for things that are gone, but we may forge new ties, new interrelations, and bonds.

Instead of suppressing our emotions, we pay attention to our wants and move, adapt, improve, and progress. We might start interacting with people and getting entangled in their affairs. We make investments in our relationships with our companions and with ourselves. We begin to exist again, but we can't until we've allowed grief permission to work on us. In this stage, you may seem more at ease speaking out with loved ones and relatives. Still, it's also normal to occasionally feel like you'd rather keep to yourself. Additionally, you could have periods of acceptance of the loss before moving on to a new stage of grief. It is usual for locations to alternate, which is how the body heals.

DOES GRIEF END AFTER THESE FIVE STAGES?

Since their inception, the stages have changed and have received much misinformation throughout the previous forty years. These stages weren't created to assist in tidying up messed-up emotions anyway. There is no average reaction to losing because there isn't a conventional loss. Yet, these are reactions to a loss that many individuals have. The structure that comprises our ability to deal with the one we lost includes the five stages. They serve as aids to enable us to categorise and name potential emotions. However, they do not represent a point in time where grief ends. Not everybody passes through them all or in the designated order. We believe that by understanding these stages and the location of grief, we will be better able to deal with life's ups and downs. Individuals who are grieving may describe more steps. Remember that your sadness is as distinct as you are, as I have always emphasised.

Among those who have built on the work of Kübler-Ross is David Kessler, who also co-authored two books with Kübler-Ross. Kessler added the stage of "finding meaning," a new location to the initial stages of Kübler-Ross in his book *"Finding Meaning: The Sixth Stage of Grief."* Let's look into that.

. . .

*F*inding meaning: many individuals look for "healing after a loss." According to Kessler, finding meaning outside the usual stages of grief, stated by Kübler-Ross, can help sorrow become a more tranquil and upbeat process. In this book, Kessler provides readers with a step-by-step guide for remembering the deceased with more admiration than sadness. He also demonstrates how to proceed in a way that respects our loved ones. The wisdom of Kessler is both profoundly practical and deeply personal. When he was a young child, and his mother faced death, he saw a shooting incident. This was the beginning of his journey through grief.

People are naturally driven to look for meaning in their lives. However, it could seem complicated to consider trying to create a more significant purpose in your life without a mom if you are filled with despair as you fight to admit the truth of their passing. However, after the initial few weeks of your mom's passing, if you can devote a brief period, across as many days as possible, to resetting your objectives and reinventing your ultimate mission. This can bring glimmers of joy, a pleasant diversion from your pain. It might aid in your greater acceptance of the loss of your loved one. You might feel more connected to your loved one who has passed away in mind if you can accept the loss more quickly.

Although grieving after the loss of a loved one is a common reaction and searching for new meaning is a universal human urge, the road to reconciled grief can be challenging. It may be helpful to consult with a psychiatric expert who focuses on grief counselling if more than a few years have elapsed since the death of your loved one. You are getting burdened or realise your grief messes with your everyday activity. They can work collaboratively with you to eliminate roadblocks so you can strike an equilibrium between the range of feelings that arise with the conflict to admitting your mom's passing, the pleasure that can result from discovering a new purpose in your life, and the tranquillity that comes from connecting with your loss.

TRIGGER DAYS: COPING WITH MEMORIES

The unpredictable nature of grieving is one of its most challenging aspects. It can occur in any place and at any moment. There will inevitably be things that bring to memory a person with whom you once spent a significant portion of your life. Occasionally, we refer to these as grief triggers. Ranging from some concrete stuff, like a particular image or music coming from the radio, to something more elusive and probably harder to escape, like the sound of rainfall, the sense of the weather changing, or the way your sibling moves like the deceased person. A trigger could be anything. You can be going about your day relatively painlessly when all of a sudden, the agony, the worry, or the sorrow resurfaces in you.

The easiest way to characterise grief triggers is as abrupt reminders of the loss of a loved one that cause strong emotional reactions in you. Interacting with grief triggers might occur due to unanticipatedly running into circumstances that bring up memories of a deceased loved one. These reminders stir powerful feelings that could send you spiralling again into your grief. A quick outburst of tears, rage, anger, confusion or intense sadness are a few more prevalent emotional reactions to grief. "I had assumed I was past this" may come to mind when you are startled by something as potent or intense as a grief trigger.

Grief may suddenly overtake you when you're going about your daily activities and having a pleasant day. While you may know that these moments would be challenging, your reaction could not become fully apparent until you go through one of these prompting events. There may be other grief triggers that snare you. Because you know that certain meals or streets will make you think of your departed one, you can dodge them. Perhaps you realise that your best course of action for dealing with them is to avoid them at all costs. Trying to manage as much of your situation as possible is a relief in and of itself. But it's crucial to remember that you will eventually come across things that make you think of your departed one, which will likely trigger some emotional discomfort.

Grief triggers are unpleasant since they let uninvited subjective emotions stream in. These emotions just come to you when you're trying to remember something. They might suddenly strike you as you walk down the road, work at your computer, or heat snacks in the microwave. Many of these emotions are unimportant, but others—particularly those connected to loved ones who have passed away—can elicit a wide range of reactions.

However, just because grieving triggers can be unanticipated doesn't imply you have no control over them. You might feel shocked and irritated if you experience abrupt sadness at an inconvenient time, such as while at work or getting ready to visit your sibling after a long time. While it's not usually easy, you can occasionally manage to keep it together until you can find a private opportunity alone. You can accumulate a set of techniques through time to aid you in getting through these particularly trying times.

The circumstances that cause your anguish and sadness to resurface tend to happen later when other forces make grieving more difficult. This is often referred to as a delayed or extended grief trigger. For instance, a person caring for a deceased parent might not become aware of the effects of the loss of their parent until after some time. They could find it difficult to concentrate on their grieving due to weariness from excessive work, care for their dying parent, and general lethargy. Even days or weeks following their parent's passing, they could not feel their loss emotionally. They may experience grief due to receiving the last cost bill in the mailbox or as a result of hospice personnel entering their house to retrieve medical items. At some stage, they come to terms with the fact that their parents are no more around and that they must now deal with life without them.

WHAT ARE THE EXAMPLES OF GRIEF TRIGGERS?

People grieving might not always be aware of the situations and events that trigger powerful sorrowful reactions. It takes time to comprehend why a particular occasion, moment, location, scent, or touch elicit negative emotional responses. Feelings are typically solid and spontaneous after a death or other loss. However, as time passes, your suffering lessens, and you begin to feel lighter. Then something triggers you, which might send your emotions into a frenzy. Here are a few typical examples of situations that may trigger your grief:

*N*ew Developments: Receiving marriage or graduation invites frequently causes emotional grieving reactions. Even if you assumed you got your grief under regulation, you might still suffer pain over your loss at these kinds of significant life events.

. . .

*S*pecial Days: Christmas, reunions, vacations, and other noteworthy events year-round can be painful for those who have lost someone close. These ongoing, lasting memes will probably cause some degree of sadness.

*F*avourite music: No matter how much time has elapsed since the passing of a loved one, a specific song composed in their honour may still cause you to experience some level of pain.

*V*oices or smells: The smell of a particular perfume or the sounds of kids playing may make you sense your loss again. Some noises and smells can take you back in time, such as your loved one's trademark fragrance, a particular cigar type, or distant youngsters giggling and playing.

a missed opportunity: Taking your mother out on mother's day, celebrating your father on father's day, and some family holidays all have a tendency to draw your notice to your loss. You can discover that these occasions emphasise your loss, especially if your parent or child passed away.

HOW DO YOU RECOGNISE YOUR TRIGGERS?

An essential part of your psychological process is realising what makes your grief appear more severe. A standard grief period can last between a few weeks and a full year. Understanding your triggers might help you deal with this trying period by using appropriate coping mechanisms. You don't have to worry about when the following triggering circumstance will occur constantly. Knowing what causes your pain will solve the struggle halfway. Understanding the causes of your feelings will help you identify effective strategies to assist you in moving past your grief.

Living and perception would not be the same for you again after the death of someone so dear to your heart. You might need some time to absorb and come to terms with the death of someone you love. Your grief may take a whole different turn as reality sinks in. You'll notice that some situations trigger your grieving reactions without instantly understanding why. Studying your triggers, the emotions they arouse in you, and appropriate coping mechanisms will help you identify your grieving triggers. Inability to recognise your grieving triggers might make you feel as though they happen unexpectedly, which can exacerbate whatever discomfort you may already be feeling from sorrow-related feelings. You may tell when your emotions are related to your sadness by using the following procedures:

- Tune in with yourself periodically during the day, and start maintaining a mindful journal to take records of your feelings.
- Be sure to record your spot, the feeling, any physical reactions, the degree of the surface on a rating, the person you were with, and every engagement you had in your mindful journal whenever you encounter a more severe mental episode during the day.
- You can start to see a trend in your triggers after some weeks.
- Remember to record cases of provoking individuals, scenarios, or events in your journal.
- Be kind to yourself and understand that it could take some moments to identify your triggers for grieving.

HOW DO YOU COPE WITH THESE MEMORIES?

For every trigger situation, there is always a way out. If your grief triggers are not bringing you some lovely memories, you must get an escape route to help you cope with these feelings. Let's discuss some things you could do to cope with grief triggers.

. . .

*I*dentify **your grief triggers:** We won't be dwelling more on this to avoid repetition. We have talked extensively about how to recognise triggers in the previous section. It is noteworthy to mention why this step is essential to you as you cope with your grief triggers.

Like many other psychological situations, the first step to healing may be admitting and identifying your grief. Putting your sentiments into words when you get a chance to sit with them can be beneficial. What mainly caused these emotions to arise? Why could you be behaving in this manner? How does grief manifest physically in you? Feeling sick to your tummy? A throat constriction? Aching in your head? It may manifest itself physically or through a string of actions. When grief unexpectedly overwhelms you, and you're unsure of why pay attention to the circumstances that led to your feelings of hopelessness. Typically, it's anything that may have made you recall a minor character of the departed soul, like a scar that wasn't obvious or their crooked feet. You'll be more able to prevent the development of sadness during inconvenient times after you get informed of a few of your triggers.

. . .

*C*onsider your triggers: It can seem contradictory to allow oneself to enjoy your emotional journey while grieving correctly. Some people may feel the impulse to suppress their feelings and disconnect from what transpired since grief can be unbearably painful. Be aware that this desire is quite normal and prevents you from feeling discomfort. However, practising so may make your suffering last longer since your mind needs time to analyse painful events before consolidating and storing memories adequately. You may frequently get triggered or exhibit signs of one or more psychological health issues if the mind cannot absorb an encounter enough.

Attempting to keep one's emotions hidden from oneself and others slows the grieving process. You'll be able to comprehend when these thoughts appear apparently out of the blue if you can embrace your grief, sentiments, and feelings. All of it is a symptom of the mourning response to loss. Feeling, accepting, and letting go of these pain surges will eventually come naturally to you. Similar to how sea waves flow in turns, when one is coming, you prepare yourself for it by anticipating the next.

· · ·

*D*evelop a plan: When you become aware of common triggers, you can start preparing for circumstances that probably result in a triggered reaction. Having designed a strategy that ensures your emotional security, you need to be conscious of your existing triggers. Be aware that based on the stage you are in the grieving cycle; your motivations may likely change. Think about different possible results for the impending triggering situation. Make a list of a few healthy coping mechanisms to have choices. If you do, you have options if you become triggered by the circumstance.

*E*stablish limits for yourself: Recognise that grieving-related feelings and ideas can be utterly draining and that there will be moments when you must stop and allow yourself some space to grieve internally. Plan some moments to enable yourself to thoroughly explore your feelings and ideas about this grief, but also make sure you are looking after yourself and giving yourself much respite to ensure you are not zoning out or separating from your emotion. Take breaks to refuel and ensure you are not constantly exhausting yourself mentally.

You can eat anything healthy during breaks even if you don't feel hungry. Keeping your body nourished is crucial even if you forget to eat frequently during this period. You might alternatively read a humorous novel or see a movie that won't cause you to experience grief-related solid feelings. You could as well communicate with family members or do mindfulness meditation.

DO YOUR GRIEF TRIGGERS NEED TO BE AVOIDED?

Each individual grieves differently in a different way. You'll have to experiment to determine what functions most for you, whether you decide to face your triggers or completely dodge them. At the outset, avoiding grief triggers isn't necessarily a terrible idea. Some individuals might use this as a healing strategy to help them navigate through the initial phases of grieving until they become more resilient and equipped to manage their feelings. Think about choosing a future occasion, like a birthday or another memorable day, to be at peace with your loss. Start psychologically bracing yourself for this occasion, and if necessary, think about asking a loved one for assistance.

Grief triggers might have some positive effects as well. Confronting our grief may be helpful and aid in our eventual acceptance of life with it. Triggers might sometimes bring back beautiful memories people wouldn't like to remember. But it depends on us when and whether we are prepared for these triggers. In the initial stages of grieving, most of us feel shocked, which can initially shield us. Shock is that state of indifference where nothing seems natural yet, and nothing seems to be happening. Throughout that phase, we may not cry or respond emotionally to triggers.

Face-to-face time with a few of our triggers can occasionally be helpful. Listening to depressing music and looking at old pictures can be cathartic for many individuals. Others are unable to face them. Each of us is aware of our needs and levels of preparedness. If you desire to stay away from your triggers, particularly if you don't wish to cry in front of others, there is no harm in doing so. When the moment is perfect for you to grieve, you'll recognise it, and you're free to do it at your own pace. Of course, some triggers can't be avoided, like anniversaries and holidays. Still, you don't have to participate if you're not prepared regarding what you can and cannot do, be assertive regarding what you can and cannot do. You'll ultimately be able to enjoy these moments once more and leverage them to relive priceless memories.

Don't be nervous about particular locations when you're prepared. Consider doing it in honour of or for the benefit of the departed soul. Recognise that even if you couldn't attend certain events for some reason, you shared the excitement and hope of going to attend. And if you made it there, cherish the memories. Try to be forgiving to anyone who might say something foolish. Due to its suddenness and lack of control, this grief trigger may be one of the most difficult to manage. This frequently causes us to become furious, which is a typical reaction when we are worried or grieving. Then, as a result of our anger, we could feel bad or humiliated about acting out. We accuse the other individual of causing us to feel this way. But if we take a step back and consider it, why should people share our perception of how we are feeling? Nobody experiences life the same way as you do. Maybe it is not unexpected that people find it challenging to communicate with us because most of us are confused and unsure of how to handle our grief.

Because our loved ones linger on in our memories long after they pass away, we keep things that serve as a reminder of them and frequent locations where they seem nearby. Indeed, we always run the possibility of experiencing pain again after losing somebody we cherish. However, on the contrary, if we allow them, these memories can also make us feel warm and cosy. In time, you might discover that the identical "grief triggers" that formerly made you unhappy now make you feel love and nostalgia.

FINDING COMFORT: CRAWLING OUT OF THE STORM

> Grief is in two parts. The first is loss. The second is the remaking of life. Anne Roiphe

It may seem as though your sadness and loss will never be fully expressed when a loved one passes away. You may go through one of the most challenging phases of your life while you grieve. Despite your sorrow, light is still at the end of the tunnel. You can crawl out of your storm and find long-lasting comfort. Finding comfort is not a one-way thing. You could find solace in yourself as someone grieving, or you could help some other person suffering find comfort. Whichever way you are doing it, ensure somebody is allowed.

You may take care of many tasks for yourself to assist you in getting beyond your grief. Below, I have provided several exercises and practices you might want to attempt. Do not feel obligated to immediately try all (or just any!) of the recommendations; some may make more meaning at different stages of your grieving process. Some may be applicable when your grief is fresh, while others may be more applicable once you have little space to process what has occurred.

LET'S START WITH HOW TO HELP YOURSELF TO CRAWL OUT OF THE STORM.

*T*raditions and rituals: Rituals serve as a method to honour and commemorate our departed loved ones and a technique to help us cope with grief. All societies have ways that are a component of the grieving procedure because they are so crucial. For instance, funeral services are a cultural practice where we bid farewell, admit the loss, or honour the humanity of the dearly departed. When a person is cremated, there is frequently a ritual in which the ashes are spread at a final resting place. In various societies, it is customary for relatives and friends to visit the grieving household to express their sympathies and discuss the deceased's manner of passing. Traditions in many societies involve bathing the departed's body as part of the preparation process. In some Western cultures, a wake is typically held after the burial. Mexico has a Day of the Dead celebration every year to remember and respect the memories of the departed.

You can create custom ceremonies to honour and commemorate your dearly departed. Checking from the psychological perspective, these practices have significance and serve two important purposes: they enable us to find a better acceptance of what has occurred and face the fact of the loss. Some individuals might decide to dedicate a tree or host a funeral ceremony at their favourite location, for instance. You might consider what would be significant to you regarding how you want to commemorate the memory of your dearly departed parent. What would you prefer to do to honour your loved one on their anniversary?

*E*xpressing your emotions: You can start to accept your loss by talking to someone about your feelings. Could you locate any close friends or relatives with whom you seem at ease discussing your feelings? Writing about your emotions in a journal is yet another effective method of expressing your feelings. Some individuals find it best to talk to a trained grief therapist to express their feelings. Remember that other individuals occasionally try to make you appear better since it is understandable. While they may have the best intentions, this could indicate that they are trying to make you feel better when you wish to talk. If you need to chat, don't be scared to tell people that you do not need their help to get well; all you need is the opportunity to be heard.

*C*reate a memory box: Some individuals feel it's crucial to preserve their emotions after losing a loved one. Making a "memory box" of objects and images that bring up memories of your departed is one option. You could, for instance, include pictures, a few of their favourite things, their favourite song, a priceless piece of apparel, notes, their favourite book, or precious objects they gave you. You may schedule a consistent time to check your memory box, possibly on their birthday, and keep it in a unique location.

*S*haring your grief's journey: Processing what has occurred might be aided by communicating about your loss and sharing your experience of loss and grieving, as I am doing right now through this book. There is frequently a lot to digest and find a way to deal with, regardless of if your loved one passed away unexpectedly or after a protracted sickness. You may experience a need, even an urgency, to share your experience and explain what occurred as your brain tries to make meaning of your loss. This may be a crucial step in digesting all the feelings you are experiencing. Writing your account from your point of view, as if you were trying to tell people what occurred, may be beneficial if you don't think you have had an opportunity to discuss what happened appropriately. Following are some suggestions to help you get started if you wish to give it a try:

- What was going on in your daily existence right before you learned about the passing of a beloved one? If they were ailing, you can describe what occurred before you knew they would pass away.
- Writing about your experiences throughout your loved one's sickness could be beneficial. You could describe how you were diagnosed, the treatments you got, and your contact with the medical team in your essay. Try to pay attention to how you have been moved, consider your feelings and ideas, and think about what it was like for you.
- What impact has your loss had on you? Consider your emotions, reactions, and how this grief impacts your life.
- Describe how you felt when you learned that a loved one had passed away. How did they pass away? What took place? People frequently recall

this experience vividly and often express disbelief. What did you do at that moment? How were you feeling? How did you act or feel?

*T*ry and deal with avoidance: When a loss occurs, it could be too hard to do anything that would bring up memories of the deceased. It is crucial to start confronting the locations and circumstances you have been dodging as days pass. To tackle this, you could begin by noting everything you have been avoiding, including individuals, events, locations, and activities. For instance, a lake where you used to fish together often with the deceased person, a takeout meal you shared, or specific individuals who bring back memories of them. Make a pyramid from your list, placing the most challenging circumstances at the top: body, mind and spirit.

Make a strategy for how and when you will begin to deal with the circumstances you have been dodging. Kindly consider asking a friend or member of your immediate family to accompany you first. You might not have to dive right in; take it slow. Being confronted with memories might be challenging, so be patient and kind to yourself.

. . .

*W*rite a letter to the departed one: Sounds absurd, right? Yeah. But this could be a potent way of getting out of your grief. Sometimes our thoughts for our loved ones are complicated; perhaps you both said or did something during their lifetime that you afterwards regretted or that was cruel. Writing to a loved one can be a beneficial tool for processing your emotions. Try to put your feelings into words and explain all you hoped you had expressed. This looks like mindful journaling, but it's not. You're writing to someone absent as though they were present.

Writing this should not pose any difficulty. First, you can say whatever you want: this is a private message, and no one else has to read it. Allow yourself to write honestly and from the heart. If you haven't had an opportunity to speak with a loved one, you can now do so. You might describe how things have gone for you after they passed, whether pleasant or terrible. You can express to them your respect and remembrance of them. The memories that mean the most to you can be shared. You are welcome to express your apologies or emotions over any problems that were not resolved. You can express your feelings to them, and you may want to mention all the various sides of who you are. Consider what you'll do with your writing once you're through. You might either dispose of it or preserve it someplace secure. There is no correct or incorrect response; be gentle to yourself and follow your gut.

*C*onnect with the various aspects of your grief: It is common to experience conflicting emotions while grieving; for example, you could feel upset and enraged one moment and then guilty and regretful the next. Since many of us are accustomed to denying or stifling our feelings, facing them may initially seem odd and unnatural. Consider each feeling a distinct aspect of yourself as a technique for dealing with them. For instance, depending on how you think about losing a loved one, you may be sad, furious, or even afraid in different parts of you. Counsellors advise individuals to discover healthy methods to experience and 'handle' their feelings, that is, to be aware of and deal with their emotions.

Our feelings can clash with one another on occasion. For instance, the portion of you that is upset can be upset at the part of you that is afraid. Another possibility is that the amount of you that seems guilty interferes with the piece that embraces what occurred. This is what you do in situations where different parts of your emotions conflict. Start by naming your various emotional components. For example, the "furious portion," "frightened portion," "depressed or sorrowful portion," "guilty portion," "admitting portion," "comfort portion," "avoidance portion," and any other portion you are conscious of that might not have been mentioned among these. Never forget that acknowledging your feelings is okay and that no sense is inappropriate.

Draw each mental portion to your heart one at a time, and pose yourself these questions:

How is this portion of me processing my loss?

What's the sensation like with this portion?

The feeling is more robust in what part of my body?

What is this emotion trying to accomplish?

Now see an intelligent and caring aspect of yourself. This portion of you genuinely cares about you and constantly has your most significant interests in mind. What would this portion of you like to communicate to the other parts of you if they were all attentive to it?

What role does this portion of you play in healing the other parts?

What is it that this portion of you wants precisely for you?

You can connect to all portions of your emotion through these questions independently.

. . .

*M*anage remorse and guilt: It's normal to feel remorse and shame when someone we love passes away. You might remember something you expressed, could not speak, or even both. Given what has occurred, occurrences that might have previously seemed insignificant might assume a new significance. Most individuals eventually figure out how to deal with these feelings. However, remorse and guilt occasionally become trapped, as if they were a circuit. This may be pretty upsetting and interfere with mourning healthily. You could start by listing your regrets in writing to crawl out of remorse and guilt. Then try to see yourself with a kind and welcoming mindset.

Everyone makes errors and feels remorse, but that part does not create the entire narrative between you and the departed soul you love. Try to step back and treat yourself with compassion, just as you would a close friend. Consider this hypothetical scenario: What would the departed fellow say to you if they heard or saw you feeling remorseful and guilty? How could they encourage you and give you solace? What advice would a knowledgeable and kind friend give you? What would you say to someone experiencing remorse and guilt if it were someone else?

You could connect with friends and relatives about how you are doing and try to hear what they say. Often, they won't be as judgmental of you as you would be of yourself.

. . .

*M*ake tough choices: You might have to make some difficult choices after losing a loved one. In the circumstance that you invested jointly, you might have to make financial adjustments or even relocate. In the beginning, even the tiniest choices can seem daunting. If your situation permits, it is frequently wise to hold off on making significant decisions until half to a full year has elapsed. If you have to make an important choice, you might need assistance to consider your options thoroughly. If you need help in coming up with a plan, think about asking a dependable friend or relative for help. A traditional approach to tackling problems is to begin by noting the nature of the problem. Then consider all of your alternatives and view all of the potential solutions. Think about the benefits and drawbacks of each option, then decide which is the most sensible and beneficial choice for everyone. Prepare what you'll need to implement your choice once you've made one.

HOW DO YOU HELP SOMEONE ELSE CRAWL OUT OF THE STORM OF GRIEF?

Talking about death and grief may be challenging, and many individuals find it hard to decide what to say while attempting to help anyone who has been grieving. You might want to assist but hesitate for fear of uttering "the inappropriate thing." Below are a few suggestions for helping someone following a loss.

*A*ccept the situation and make contact instead of avoiding it. Even while it's reasonable to feel awkward talking about a tragedy or other losses or to fear that you might utter the inappropriate thing, keeping quiet or avoiding someone after their grief can frequently exacerbate emotions of loneliness and despair. It can be beneficial to get in touch with the grieving individual and let them know you're willing to hear them and discuss with them if they'd like.

*T*hink about the best way to communicate. After a death, there are several ways to speak and various grieving approaches. Someone might find handling incoming texts and emails simpler than making callbacks. For some, stopping to visit them in person may be pleasant, but it may be inconvenient for many. Instead of assuming what someone would like, it is essential to ask them.

. . .

*E*nsure you allow enough space for grief processing. It may be worthwhile to let grieving individuals realise they can reply anytime they feel ready or give messages in the form of texts or mail to notify them that you are concerned about them and that response is unnecessary. Grieving individuals may not like to devote much time to other folks or feel bad for not confirming message receipts. Grieving individuals should be given the opportunity and privacy to absorb their feelings for however long they deem necessary because adjusting to living after a loss might take much time. It's helpful if you can find a happy medium between reaching out to them and letting them have some privacy so they don't feel alone. Once more, asking them which they would prefer is a great idea.

*D*iscuss the deceased person. It may seem as though a deceased person's memories are buried with them when they pass away. Even though you might be afraid that discussing the dead person will only evoke negative emotions, many individuals value the chance to share a few memorable moments of the individual because they find it to be comforting. It can be helpful to ask, "What's your favourite moment with [the deceased]?" or to say, "discuss with me a moment when [the deceased] made you smile." A means to integrate the recent memories of the dearly departed into their hearts instead of repressing memories.

*C*onsider listening. Endeavour to honour the grieving person's decision to communicate with you and emphasise listening more than knowing more. Provide the individual grieving room to express themselves if they wish to, but be understanding if they'd prefer not.

*P*ay attention to the person who has lost a loved one. Instead of returning to your thoughts about the loss, endeavour to maintain the conversation with the grieving individual. Similarities with your circumstances might not be beneficial if you haven't personally gone through grief.

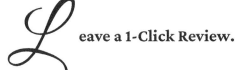

eave a 1-Click Review.

Customer reviews

☆☆☆☆☆ 5 out of 5

4 global ratings

5 star	▓▓▓▓▓▓	100%
4 star		0%
3 star		0%
2 star		0%
1 star		0%

ˇ How customer reviews and ratings work

Review this product

Share your thoughts with other customers

Write a customer review

I would be incredibly grateful if you could take just 60 seconds of your valuable time to write a brief review on Amazon, even if it's just a few words.

POST SCRIPT LIVING AFTER

Grief frequently seems like it hits in strong, overpowering waves at first. These grieving waves may seem to appear from nowhere or may be brought on by memories of the individual you lost. When you initially lose somebody, it may appear as if you are getting battered by colossal waves of sadness, occasionally coming so close that you can barely catch your breath. The magnitude of the waves tends to diminish over time as the intervals between them widen.

You may encounter countless "firsts" as you learn to explore life in the absence of the departed soul over the following days, weeks, and months. Examples of this may include your first Christmas in the absence of your mother, your first birthday after your father's death, your first mother's day after the loss, and so on. It will be normal to notice their failure in any of these circumstances, re-igniting previous waves of sorrow.

Friends and family members' desire to encourage you is entirely understandable. But occasionally, you could discover how other individuals react to you isn't always beneficial. For example, other folks can experience discomfort and be at a loss for words. Some people find it challenging to redirect the conversation from their grief and move on. Some others could even avoid you. Some may be prepared for you to improve and continue before you're ready.

On the other hand, some people may not understand how to react as you expect. Some are not sure if they could say stuff like, "hope you have gotten over it?" Some might desire to discuss it with you inordinately.

Keep in mind that it's acceptable to communicate your needs and wants to others. While grieving, you can experience ups and downs in your desire to share. In other instances, all you might desire to do is discuss how you're feeling and seek escape from the situation. It may be unclear to you and the other person what you require from them. Always remember that there are no regulations and that it's okay to feel whichever way.

Even when a loved one has passed away physically, their memory and spirit can live on in your thoughts and memories. For each individual, this may be carried out differently. For instance, it can imply that you keep saying goodbye to them and still fill them in on your daily routines, that you keep on with several of your shared rituals and activities, or that you visit their favourite location on their birthday.

It can be challenging even to want to live again and look for methods to be joyful when a soul has experienced a significant loss. Many individuals will attempt it when the moment is perfect. It's likely not going to be simple, and some mornings will be more excellent than others. Even with this challenging navigation, you can still make it out alive and return to your usual original self. This won't happen overnight, but I assure you that you can find meaning and purpose again. I have been there, and I am living testimony to this. This offering is just one of my ways of finding fulfilment again after life has dealt me, plus its colossal blow. I hope it will help you to crawl out of the raging storm of life and again find your feet in vitality and normalcy.

A SPECIAL GIFT FOR YOU

𝒶 FREE GIFT TO OUR READERS

5 Daily Meditations that you can use to guide you past your grieving. These meditations are very impactful and complement this book to give you comfort, hope and inspiration on your potential to be your best after losing your loved one. You can download and start using it now! Visit this link

https://bit.ly/3dXpPAr

BIBLIOGRAPHY

David Kessler. (2019). *Finding meaning; The sixth stage of grief.* New York, NY: Scribner, 2020. ©2019. 9781501192746.

Erika Krull (2022). *Grief By The Numbers: Facts and Statistics.* The Recovery Village. Retrieved on 19/07/22 from https://www.therecoveryvillage.com/mental-health/grief/grief-statistics/

Forbes Health. (2022). Marissa Conrad. *What Is Anticipatory Grief, And How Does It Work?* Retrieved 20/07/22 from https://www.forbes.com/health/mind/what-is-anticipatory-grief/

Harbor Light Hospice (2020). *What Does a Coma Feel Like?* Retrieved 24/07/22 from https://www.harborlighthospice.com/blog/what-does-a-coma-feel-like/

Kübler-Ross E (1969). *On Death and Dying.* Routledge. ISBN 0-415-04015-9.

Mary-Frances O'Connor (2022). *The Grieving Brain: The Surprising Science of How We Learn from Love and Loss.* An imprint of Harper Collins Publishers.

MILNE Library. *Care at the Time of Death.* Retrieved 25/07/22 from https://milnepublishing.geneseo.edu/nursingcare/chapter/care-at-the-time-of-death/

Mostofsky E., Maclure M., Sherwood J.B., Tofler G.H., Muller J.E., MD, and Mittleman M.A., (2012) *Risk of Acute Myocardial Infarction After the Death of a Significant Person in One's Life.* Published 9 Jan 2012https://doi.org/10.1161/CIRCULATIONAHA.111.061770Circulation. 2012;125:491–496

Osterweis M, Solomon F, Green M, (1984). Editors. CHAPTER 5, *Bereavement During Childhood and Adolescence.* Institute of Medicine (US) Committee for the Study of Health Consequences of the Stress of Bereavement; Bereavement: Reactions, Consequences, and Care. Washington (DC): National Academies Press (US).

Medical News Today. (2020). What are catecholamines, and what do they do? Medically reviewed by Alana Biggers, MD, MPH — Written by Anna Smith. Retrieved online on 27/07/22 from https://www.medicalnewsto day.com/articles/catecholamines

Pamela Li. (2022). *How Does The Death Of A Parent Affect A Child?* Parenting For Brain. Retrieved online on 26/07/22 from https://www.parentingfor brain.com/death-of-a-parent/

Vedantu. *Rigor Mortis.* Retrieved 25/07/22 from https://www.vedantu.com/ biology/rigor-mortis

Worden, J. W. (1991). Grief counselling and grief therapy: A handbook for the mental health practitioner (2nd edition). London: Springer.

30 Comforting Loss of Mother Quotes for People Who Are Missing Their Moms Today

https://www.goodhousekeeping.com/holidays/mothers-day/g20140930/ loss-of-mother-quotes/?slide=3

Made in the USA
Monee, IL
16 October 2022